SILVER B
COMPAI

G000150365

Edited by

TONY ORTZEN

The Spiritual Truth Press

First published in 1986
Reprinted 1995
This edition 1999

The Spiritual Truth Press
15 Broom Hall, Oxshott
Surrey KT22 0JZ

ISBN 0 85384 095 4

Printed in Great Britain by Booksprint

Foreword

There are a number of possible reasons why you are reading this book. The first and most likely is that you are already a 'follower' of Silver Birch and have found his great wisdom and spiritual insights of benefit in your life. In this case you will welcome this reprint of one of the classic books of his teachings. Maybe you have been given this book by a friend who believes its message of love, in this world and the next, will inspire or comfort you. If so, you will not be dissappointed.

Perhaps you chanced upon it on a bookshelf or saw it advertised, then curiosity got the better of you. Well, after reading its pages you may also decide that 'chance' played no part in the decision and that some form of spiritual guidance has brought you and this book together.

Whatever the reason, the chances are that Silver Birchs's wisdom will remain with you forever. Long after you have forgotten his precise words, his guidance will still be a very real influence whenever you need it. And if you need to jog your memory - just reach for this book and read it again. Silver Birch's words are so accessible and meaningful that you will never tire of reading them. But who is Siver Birch, the spirit guide whose words are faithfully recorded here? And who was Maurice Barbanell, the London medium who channelled that wisdom? Without an answer to these qestions, many new readers - however impressed with these teachings - will be puzzled about their source.

Barbanell was the founder and editor of a weekly Spiritualist newspaper, *Psychic News*, and for half a century devoted his life to spreading spiritual knowledge through its columns and those of other publications with which he was associated. In his own obituary, which he wrote before his passing at the age of 79 on July 17th 1981, he revealed that he was told by Estelle Roberts' Red Cloud - a spirit guide for whom he had the greatest admiration - that in a previous incarnation he had made a promise to reincarnate and devote his life to spreading Spiritualism. Though he had no knowledge of that life or promise, events certainly conspired to make it possible.

He was born to Jewish parents in a poor area of London's East End. His mother was devoutly religious but his father, a barber, was an atheist so Barbanell heard many arguments about religion during his early years. His father always won, and his son adopted the same outlook but later changed to agnosticism. Yet after hearing about Spiritualism from a speaker at a social and literary club of which he was secretary, Barbanell refused to start the debate by putting an opposing view - one of his duties - because, he explained, he had made no personal investigation and therefor his opinions were valueless. This impressed the speaker who invited Barbanell to attend a sceance in which a medium, Mrs Blaustein, was entranced by various spirits of different nationalities. He was not impressed, and on a second visit fell asleep. Barbanell apologised, believing that either boredom or tiredness had been responsible, but the other circle members informed him that he had not been asleep but had been in trance and a Red Indian had spoken through him.

With the enccouragement of famous Fleet Street journalist Hannen Swaffer, Barbanell founded *Psychic News* partly as a vehicle for the guide's teachings. But, because he knew he would be criticised for publishing his own mediumship in his own newspaper, Barbanell did not reveal to his readers for many years who was channelling the wisdom, by which time the guide had a huge following on his own merits.

Silver Birch spoke regularly at Barbanell's home circle and the proceedings were always recorded in shorthand. There were a number of diffferences in style and procedure between Barbanell's own journalistic efforts and the way in which Silver Birch communicated, as Barbanell himself observed: "In my working life I use words every day. I have never yet written or dictated an article with which I was satisfied when I read it. Inevitably I find, when looking at the typed material, that I can improve it by altering words, phrases and sentences. No such problem arises with the guide's teachings. These flow perfectly, requiring usually only punctuation. Another interesting aspect is the occasional use of words that I regard as archaic and do not form part of my normal vocabulary."

But who was Silver Birch? A psychic artist depicts him as a serious-looking native American Indian with a single feather and compassionate eyes. There is evidence to suggest that this was simply a convenient *persona* behind which a far more spiritually-evolved soul hid in order that those who read his words would judge them not by the name attached to them but by the wisdom that pervades every sentence.

Those of us who knew both were well aware of the differences in the way they spoke and the words they used. They both had spiritual missions and they fulfilled them admirably, particularly when working together in their unique two-world partnership. This, as you are about to discover, has provided us with simple, uplifting, comforting and inspirational answers to the questions we all ask, from time to time, about life and its purpose. They are needed now more than ever before as we prepare for the challenges that will confront us in the 21st century.

Roy Stemman
Chairman
Spiritual Truth Foundation

CONTENTS

I F you are wedded to ancient fable, to old belief, or if you have reached the summit of spiritual knowledge, do not read this book. But if you recognise that life is an adventure, that the soul constantly searches for new fields to traverse, new avenues to explore, then here you will find those fundamental truths of the spirit which are behind all the religions of the world.

There is naught here contrary to that which was taught by the founders of all religions. Here is contained the truth concerning life on earth and life hereafter. If you are ready to receive it, you will find it will illumine your mind and enrich your soul. There is nothing here that will make your reason revolt or will insult your intelligence, for all is presented in the spirit of love and the desire to serve.

Silver Birch

INTRODUCTION

IT was a Friday night: the working week was at an end. The phone rang in my then home in up and coming Islington, North London. "He's gone," said famous spirit healer M. H. Tester, a director of Psychic Press and close friend of Maurice Barbanell, Silver Birch's medium. "Gone? Gone to hospital?" I replied. "No! He's been taken." "Taken where?" I queried.

Then I realised the full impact of Mr Tester's words. Though I had given up smoking some weeks previously, my hand reached nervously for an unopened packet and lit up a cigarette. It was the first of many over the next few hours and long, long into a night silent except for my typewriter and the occasional passing car. For none of our lives would ever be the same again. July 17, 1981, was a turning point from which there could be no retreat or return. Something bigger than all of us seemed to be running events. We were for the time being but pawns on the chessboard of life and death.

Having alerted various colleagues I went to the offices of "Psychic News." My heart felt heavy, my face slightly flushed. Yet this was no time for contemplation or reflection. There were phone calls to be made, telegrams to be sent, a paper to redesign. Arriving home some weary hours later, I sat at my desk and in the early hours of the morning with solitude for once a welcome companion wrote Maurice Barbanell's obituary. I felt humble that one so young should find this task allotted to him unasked, unsought.

Previously that evening I opened the safe at "Psychic News" and read the account of his own life and psychic quest written by Maurice Barbanell. For over 60 years he occupied a ringside seat at seances and psychic events, earning himself the nickname "Mr Spiritualism." Now he was in the spirit world he did so much to champion, extol and defend. So it was I recalled the first time I saw the self-written obituary some years beforehand. "The next time I see this," I then thought, "the Old Man will have gone."

Now he had. His spirit was free, his physical body at rest. Strangely enough only weeks before The Boss, as he was affectionately known at work, had told me several things about his early life. It seemed almost unbelievable that never again would I and my editorial colleagues see him completing a crossword—sometimes giving me a thorny clue to crack—lighting up one of his familiar, pungent, outsize cigars, packing his briefcase or wandering down the street on his way to a sandwich bar. Suddenly a light had gone out. Sleep was but fitful and unrefreshing on that July night. I felt desperately alone, unsure and uncertain. A door had closed. What lay in front of the now depleted team at "Psychic News" none of us knew . . .

I first met Maurice Barbanell when I was a young journalist of 20. I had come to London some weeks previously, moved into a flat with friends and started job-hunting. In sheer desperation I took a job as a filing clerk, with its monotonous duties: truly did I discover what it was to be the lowest form of life in a busy commercial office. But there are times in one's life when Fate takes a hand and unbidden beckons one forth.

Let me explain. The American oil company for which I worked decided to start an in-house paper. Discovering I was a college-trained journalist with over two years' experience on an award-winning weekly newspaper, I was summoned to the personnel officer's office and asked if I would like to help establish the journal. No matter that I did not then know anything about layout: an agency would see to that side. The salary certainly was not to be scoffed at. Neither were the opportunities for travel. Names like Scandinavia and the Far East dropped from the personnel officer's lips.

But the day was yet young. Fate continued to look on . . . and provided two more and two very different signposts. Previously I was interviewed at an employment agency. What it sought were interviewers to help job applicants. And on that day—a Wednesday—came a letter offering me a job as an interviewer at one of its offices.

Yet even more was in store. Maurice Barbanell, knowing of my interest in Spiritualism, wrote asking me to go and see him. Would I phone to make an appointment? Mr Barbanell was somewhat evasive when I rang, but I half-guessed he might offer me a job. He did. So on that one day I had three very different jobs staring me in the face. The one at "Psychic News" was certainly the worst paid. I had no idea what the long term prospects were. To be frank, with the slight arrogance that many a youth suffers from I found "Psychic News" a trifle dated and inward-looking. Nonetheless, there was no doubt within my mind which position I would accept. Some 14 or 15 years later, older and a lot wiser, I am still at "Psychic News," now as editor.

Maurice Barbanell taught me a great deal, not only about journalism but also about life. Because there was a 50-year age difference between us we sometimes seemed to have what one might call a grandfather-grandson relationship. Often I said things slightly out of place: he would look through his strong spectacles, but usually say little to scold, perhaps putting my youthful naiveté or temerity down to inexperience. At work he was formal, sometimes painfully so. Most, except a select few, had to call him Mr Barbanell, and not by his nickname of Barbie. All those in the editorial office had to ask every night at 5.30pm if they could go home. In the end this was reduced to such a fine art I would merely poke my head around his office door: Mr Barbanell, saying nothing, would smile and wave. I could go.

None worked harder than he. Maurice Barbanell was the first to arrive—and the last to leave. Often he showed me small but telling kindnesses, like giving me cigarettes on my birthday. Neither shall I ever forget how he took me out for a lunchtime drink when I reached the then magical age of 21. Maurice Barbanell drank but rarely, and never entered a pub. Yet on this occasion he did. I can picture him now, a small, dapper figure ordering a tomato juice and cheese sandwich "without pickle." And his birthday present that time was to invite me to hear Silver Birch for the first time.

In times of personal crises and difficulty he often reached out, offering a helping hand and wise counsel. But the times I got to know him best were on Tuesdays, travelling back to London after a day in Essex at the printers. Now and again he would talk of his young days in London's harsh East End: about the bed bugs which plagued the small, cramped family flat: how his father practised "dentistry" in the young Barbanell's bedroom: about the time he got drunk once . . . and never again! Then he would reminisce affectionately about his old friend Hannen Swaffer, the eccentric "Pope of Fleet Street," who was known for his three "isms," Spiritualism, Socialism and journalism. What a strange pair they must have made: the small, snappily dressed Barbanell and the tall, peculiar-looking Swaffer, who often wore black and a cravat to boot.

This very day I have been to the Barbanells' former flat in St John's Wood, North-west London. How sad it was to see their once so smart apartment looking almost empty and dejected. For it was in that Upper Room, so to speak, that for decades Silver Birch imparted his words of wisdom.

To return to July 17, 1981, that Fateful Friday, Maurice Barbanell, who was simply never ill, had returned from his usual three-week holiday abroad. He spoke of a slight chest infection. Though he looked tanned, Mr Barbanell would gasp now and again to catch his breath. He complained about a pounding heart. On the Wednesday he went home early, instructing me—then assistant editor at "Psychic News"—to use his office should he not be in the next day. Ofttimes happenings stand out and prove that coming events do cast their shadows. This was such a case. Previously I had planned, and gained permission, to emigrate permanently to Australia. On that Friday a photographer from "Australasian Express" turned up to photograph me to illustrate an article I had written for that paper. For the pictures I sat in Maurice Barbanell's office, in his chair, at his desk.

By the end of that day I was acting editor for the founder of "Psychic News" had quit the earthly scene. In retrospect I should not have been surprised. I phoned Maurice Barbanell but two hours before he passed to assure him that the paper was all right; pages had been sent down to the printers; we were coping. "Tony," he said, "I'm so sorry. I am so very, very sorry." I have since heard those words many times in my mind. The result is always the same: an involuntary shiver running all over me.

It is impossible to measure the comfort and upliftment Silver Birch's words have brought to a sorely troubled, unpredictable and turbulent world. "Silver Birch Companion" is based upon two much earlier books, "Wisdom of Silver Birch" and "More Teachings of Silver Birch." Fittingly the second of these was compiled by Sylvia Barbanell. They were published in 1941 and 1944 respectively. But the ensuing years have not detracted from their value or worth for Silver Birch's teachings are eternal. They cannot date simply because truth does not date. It is permanent, meant for all peoples, in all times, in all cultures. Silver Birch is a skilled communicator: his oratory is superb, his choice of vocabulary masterful.

This book honours not only him. It similarly honours

Maurice Barbanell and his faithful, devoted wife Sylvia. These servants of the spirit were, are and shall remain valiant souls. They toiled long and hard in their section of the vineyard. Maurice Barbanell had his faults: we all do. Many is the time he said to me, "a camel cannot see its own hump." But he played his vital part in The Plan without fear or favour: from an East End lad he worked his way up to found and edit a newspaper which seeks to educate a sometimes ugly world that there is no death. Together guide and medium reached countless peoples around the globe. In unison they brought hope to those with a weary, troubled heart, a glimmer of light to the dark, serenity, tranquillity and certainty where there was turmoil and doubt.

Now they are together in the spirit world. Their immediate earthly mission is complete. Long may they enjoy the spirit world's beauties, the bounties of the Beyond and the knowledge that they served with stout heart, resolution and conviction. Guide and medium, go safely on your continuing journey. Our love, respect and admiration are with you.

Tony Ortzen

Chapter One

'THE COIN OF SERVICE'

THROUGHOUT Silver Birch's superb teachings run many fine threads. Often he stressed the need for service. Perhaps he was trying to convey that it is so easy to pay mere lip service to such a noble attribute rather than making a practical, everyday effort.

In latter years the Hannen Swaffer Home Circle met monthly, except for a summer break. After removing his watch and glasses, Maurice Barbanell, the medium's guide, would settle down on a sofa—his wife beside him—and quietly but quickly surrender his physical body for an hour or so. On one occasion the guide told those present never to refuse any opportunity to serve, "no matter in what field you are called upon to labour." He continued:

Is not that the lesson we have been striving to teach you for so long? Have we not sought to demonstrate that service is the coin of the spirit, the only wealth that it possesses, and that it desires to share with all? Knowledge always brings responsibility. How often have you heard that said by me? The responsibility is that you shall use this knowledge wisely and well. Those who live in my world do not come back to you only so that it should gladden your hearts, but that this return from another life should act as a spur, an incentive, that it should quicken you and make you feel the desire to render service to others. Not all are called on to speak from platforms, to demonstrate the gifts of the spirit to multitudes, to a few, or in the privacy of their homes. The opportunities for service come to all those who desire to help. The love which compels those who live in our world to manifest to you is the same love that they seek to kindle in your hearts so that, expressing it, you too can manifest its qualities, its beauties, to others who need it badly.

Look around your world of to-day and see the many aching, troubled, sorrowing hearts, those who shed tears of sadness, those who are weary and perplexed, those who have lost their way, those who find that the foundations of their faith have been shattered, those who have lost all their possessions, those who know not where to turn, those who think they are without guidance, without help and without hope. Realise that the field of labour is large and the opportunities for service are many. Then, too, look at all those who still wear their fetters, who still live in their self-erected prisons of creed, dogma, ritual and ceremony. We have to teach them how to find freedom, how to liberate themselves.

There is a countless number of human beings spread throughout your whole world who badly need the service of the ones who possess knowledge. Wherever there are individuals clinging to falsity, to blindness, to superstition, to intolerance, to the dross of materialism, there is a field of service. As long as there are children of the Great Spirit ignorant of spiritual truth, you know there is work for you and for us. That is the mission on which we are all engaged. We seek to spread truth, so that all may live in the beauty of its splendour and cast the darkness caused by foibles and superstition and ignorance behind them.

There are many enemies to be destroyed in this battle, which has raged for centuries. But we are victorious, for the hosts of those who oppose us dwindle year by year. Man cannot be kept prisoner, for ever in the darkness. His soul yearns for the light. The spirit which is divine within him is restless; it demands freedom, liberty; it finds bondage irksome. That is why you must continue to present spiritual truths with all your vigour.

That is why you must hold the ideal of truth, knowing that in the end it will be accepted. That is why you must bear with the taunts of your foolish enemies, the persecution that they seek to impose on you, the ridicule and the sarcasm which are directed against you. These cannot touch you, unless you allow them to do so; they should pass you by. For with malice towards none, but with love towards all, you must conquer and you must triumph.

That is the key-note of all spirit teaching, and you must get it implanted in your minds. Whether it is a book that you write, whether it is a word of sympathy or kindness, whether it is a handshake, whether it is helping a lame dog over a stile, whether it is a silent gift that smooths someone's difficulties— the coin of service must always be yours to give.

Another time Silver Birch described himself as "a voice crying out in the wilderness." He continued: "What does it matter who I am? Judge me by what I strive to do. If my few words, my earnestness, my determination, my mission among you, bring comfort or light to one who is struggling in darkness, then I am happy."

This was the reply of Silver Birch when one of his circle asked him for a hint of his real identity. The guide revealed he was a Red Indian, that he was an evolved messenger of an advanced group who used the astral body of an Indian as a stepping stone between his own exalted sphere and ours.

"I am but a humble servant," he once said, "an interpreter for those who have sent me to expound forgotten laws that must be revived as part of the New World that is gradually dawning. Think of me always as a mouthpiece. I represent the voice of the spirit that seeks to make its presence felt in your world and which is succeeding in increasing measure. There is a vast concourse, all with wills perfectly attuned, with minds in harmony, with souls all at one. They use me, even as I use this instrument, to tell your world the truths that have been buried for too long but which are now being restored and given their rightful place in the lives of thousands of men and women."

"To us you are a very real person, not just a representative voice," said one sitter.

"I do not mean to say that I have no individuality," said Silver Birch, "for I have. But in our life co-operation is the law. We work according to a Plan, each contributing what he possesses for the common good. There are no high or low, except the spiritual attainments that each individual has won for himself. The gifts you have developed, the faculties you have evolved, these are freely given for the service of the less fortunate, so that in turn they too may offer what they possess to others less fortunate than themselves. And so the mighty chain of spirit influence, link after link, stretches from the lowest reaches of the earth to the highest points in the heavens."

"It would be very wonderful if things on earth were done in that way," remarked a sitter.

"They will be," declared the guide, "for inevitably the laws of the Great Spirit must be expressed. Those who stand in the way can hinder and delay, but they cannot prevent their maturity."

On another occasion, Silver Birch said of himself: "I have tried to show myself as your friend, guardian and guide. I wanted you to feel that I was near you, that whatever qualities I might possess they did not prevent me from enjoying a close personal touch with you, that I was interested in your problems and your difficulties and ready to give you personal help and guidance if I could.

"Remember I am not only a teacher, seeking to teach eternal truths and reveal the powers of the spirit: I am also the friend of each one of you, for I love you dearly and strive always to help you with all the strength and power that I possess. Come to me always with your difficulties, no matter what they be. If I can help you, I will do so. If I cannot, I will strive to give you strength to bear whatever cross you may be called upon to carry.

"In all my years in the world of spirit, in all the years I have spent in evolution, equipping my soul, whatever I have earned, whatever I have received, is always given freely to you with a loving heart, a willing mind, only hoping that the Great Spirit will permit me to give you all that I have. I do this so that you may realise how much I love you all, how much I serve you, how much strength I would seek to give you, so that you might always realise that the power that is behind you is a power that is divine in its purpose, a power that seeks only to bring you richness and the fruits of the spirit. Love actuates all that we seek to do, and our only aim is to manifest our love, which comes from the Great Spirit, for you all.

"We ask for no credit, no thanks, no gratitude. If we can serve; if we can see peace instead of war; smiling, happy faces instead of tears; healthy bodies instead of bodies racked with disease and pain; if we can see misery vanquished; if we can see all the despair that infests dispirited beings driven away, then we rejoice because we know that our mission is succeeding."

Silver Birch always expressed the affection of himself and those who accompanied him for the members of the circle. Before the sittings stopped on one occasion for the summer months, he stated:

"Although we cease for a while, we will be with you all, silent yet near, striving always to bring you what inspiration, power and guidance we possibly can. When the activities of the day are hushed, and in the silence of the night, your souls come into their own and you leave behind the discordant vibrations of the material world and enter—for a short time, it is true—your real homes; then we taste together some of the joys which one day will be your constant experience.

"But even when we are separated by the thin veil of matter which we can pierce because of the power that has been built, we want you to know that we are always with you, seeking to protect you with all our love. Be strong in the knowledge that the power which we bring you is the power that belongs to the highest force in life. We are but servants seeking to serve the Great Spirit by serving you who are the nearest and dearest to us.

"Think not of me just as a voice that speaks to you in the darkness for a few moments, but as a living, pulsating presence that is always round and about you, seeking to bring you whatever is best for your unfoldment and evolution. I shall miss speaking to you in the fashion that you know best in your material consciousness, but nonetheless I will be present all the time. Call on me if you desire my help and I will freely give it if it lies in my power, for you know that there is no sacrifice I would not willingly make to serve each one of you.

"Take advantage of the summer, when tree and flower, mountain and sea, bird and beast, field and river and stream reveal themselves in all their beauty. Praise the Great Spirit, Who has brought you such an infinite variety of His artistry as displayed in nature's handiwork. Seek communion with those forces; strive to find the Great Spirit as He is expressed in the silence of the forest, in the lulling of the wind, in the trilling of the bird, in the nodding pine, in the ebb and flow of the ocean, in the perfume and scent of the flower, in the drone of the insect.

"Try to learn how to become at one with nature's hidden forces, so that you can obtain through them the strength that resides there. The Great Spirit can talk to you in many ways, not only in churches and temples, through inspired prophets and mediums, through sacred books with their countless revelations, but also through the voice of nature, which is His servant. I want to convey to you the love of the Great Spirit, as expressed by all His powers—those that speak and those that are silent."

Silver Birch closed this memorable sitting by recounting the principles that guided him in his work with the circle and, through them, for the world.

"I have striven to serve you, to bring you closer together in bonds of love," he said. "I have tried to teach you of the laws of a higher realm, of a greater life. I have striven so that you might know more of your own beings, how wondrously you have been fashioned. I have also tried to teach you of your own responsibilities, so that you might know that with Truth comes the responsibility of using it in service. I have taught you to look beyond the formalism of religious ceremony, so that you could get at the real kernel of all religion, which is to give service to those who need it. And in a world that is full of despair, full of weariness, full of doubt and difficulty, I have striven to reveal those truths which will help you to help others to find the precious knowledge which spells happiness to all humanity.

"I have never encouraged baseness; I have never expressed condemnation of any individual. I have tried to expound love in its highest form. I have always appealed to your reason and to your intelligence, insisting that the truths we teach are capable of the most rigorous examination and the searchings of the mind. I am grateful for the wealth of love that has come to me, and I pray to the Great Spirit that I may continue to merit that affection which you have shown me and which has made it easier for me to perform my task.

"We call a halt and will pick up the threads presently. I shall look forward with eager anticipation to the time when we all meet once more. I leave you, as far as this body is concerned, but my spirit never leaves you. If shadows cross your path, if troubles lie upon you, if doubt stirs within your mind and perplexity finds a dwelling place within you, remember these are not realities, they are but husks. Give them wings and send them speedily forth on their flight.

"Remember, you are the Great Spirit; the Great Spirit is each one of you. The mighty force that set the whole universe in motion and created every manifestation of life, both animate and inanimate, the mighty power that fashioned the stars and the planets, the sun and the moon; the mighty force that brought life to your world of matter; the mighty force that gave your consciousness a portion of His spirit; the mighty force that is revealed in the perfect laws that control every phase of His manifestation—that power cannot fail you if you do not fail it. Let that be your strength, your refuge and your harbour, and know that always the cloak of divine love is about you and the infinite embrace holds you in its arms.

"I, whom you call Silver Birch, say farewell."

'We thank Thee for the gift of life'

"Oh, Great White Spirit, Thy infinite and wondrous laws sustain us all. Thy love holds us all in its embrace. Thy wisdom guides us. Thy power sustains us. Thy knowledge lights the torch of truth for faltering feet.

"We thank Thee for all that we know concerning Thee and Thy manifestations in the realms of spirit and in the smaller world of matter. We thank Thee for the knowledge of Thy perfect law, for that rhythm of perfection which sustains all and contains all, which faultlessly and ceaselessly sustains the whole universe and everything which dwells in it.

"Oh, Great White Spirit, we thank Thee for all the revelations of Thyself which Thou has given us at all times. We thank Thee for the willing servants who have ministered to Thy children of matter and who have sought to uplift them and to draw their eyes to those spiritual truths which alone can teach them how to live their lives in the fulness which Thou hast intended.

"Oh, Great White Spirit, who can measure the infinity of Thy wisdom, the perfection of Thy law, the supremacy of Thy knowledge, the eternity of Thy truth? Thou art wiser than the wisdom of all the ages; Thou art more mighty than human minds can comprehend; Thy spirit, which Thou hast placed within all, which enables us to live and to function, eludes the mind of man, which cannot measure it or fathom it.

"We thank Thee for the gift of life, which binds us all with one another and which makes us one vast family, which unites us spirit to spirit, heart to heart, mind to mind, and love to love, across even the gulf of 'death.'

"We thank Thee for the chain of human spirits, which is encircled by spirits released from the bodies of matter, of whom Thou art the centre.

"Great White Spirit, we pray that each one of us shall draw closer and closer to Thee, feeling the fulness of the benediction of Thy power, knowing that we are linked with Thee for eternity, that we can raise ourselves up to receive more of Thee, more of Thy wisdom, more of Thy power, so that, with our eyes fixed on the spiritual, we can learn eternal truths, and can serve Thee better."

Chapter Two

'DEATH SPELLS FREEDOM'

THERE are few certainties in life. Indeed there is only one certain fact: that those born upon this earth will one day vacate their physical bodies. Some will pass on young, often in seemingly tragic circumstances. Others will live their "three score years and ten" . . . and perhaps even beyond that.

Death, of course, can be a painful experience even for those blessed with knowledge of the afterlife. At one circle gathering Silver Birch compared passing on with the changing seasons of the year. Here, in his own unaltered words, is what he said:

"To some, the truths that I bring are elementary, because they have heard them so often. To others they are revolutionary. We are dealing with mankind at different stages of growth. Some will quarrel with what we have to say. Some will deny it. Others will object because it comes from one who is regarded as a savage by your cultured, Western world, so proficient in the arts of destruction. But the truth will stand because it is truth. Remember, what you already accept as normal is to others the greatest revolution that has ever come to mankind. We come always with the simple message that man is a spiritual being, part of the Great Spirit, linked with the Great Spirit for all eternity.

"That tie can never be dissolved. It can be weakened or strengthened, but can never be broken. Man can rise or fall, become god-like or bestial. He can use his free will to mar or to improve, but whatever he does he is forever God and God is forever him. These truths are not meant only for recital in churches, but for application to daily life, so that hunger, starvation, unemployment, disease, dirty houses and everything that is a disgrace to your civilisation may be swept on one side as an insult to the Great Spirit within human beings.

"Our message is intended for all humanity, for no matter at what stage it now is, there is sufficient for it to grasp, understand and assimilate. As mankind places its feet on the ladder of progress, so we wait at the next rung, and the rung beyond that, as he gradually climbs and claims his higher destiny."

When mention came of a bereavement sustained by one whom Silver Birch had met, the guide said: "How I wish that your eyes were not holden; how I wish that your ears were unstopped; how I wish that you could see beyond the material confines; how I wish that you could indeed know that the world in which you live is one of shadows and unreality; how I wish you could see what lies behind and could become aware of all the forces that are ceaselessly at work, striving to help you. How I wish you could see the many—your own and those who are attracted to you by service—who stand beside you. Your world is a world of shadows, it is not the substance.

"Much of our work is achieved, not through instruments such as this, though we are happy to make ourselves known and to manifest according to the ways of your own world. Unseen, unheard, we do reach you, exercising a silent but yet real influence in your lives, guiding you, quickening you, striving to direct you, aiding you to make the right choice so that your characters will grow, your souls will evolve and you will be led into those paths which will enable you to extract from life all that is necessary for your growth and understanding."

A picturesque description of death as part of the cycle of life was given by Silver Birch when, one Easter-time, he drew a comparison with the seasons of the year.

"Think of the miracle of the seasons," he said, "the eternal circle for ever revolving with unbroken constancy—the snows of winter, when all life sleeps; the herald of spring, when life awakens; the fulness of summer, when life is revealed in all its beauty; autumn, when the voice of nature is hushed and preparation is made for sleep ere the period of refreshment comes upon it.

"You are about to witness nature's great revelation—spring, Easter, resurrection—when the new life makes itself visible all over your world, the life that has been sleeping, the life that has retreated into the darkness of mother earth, there to find peace and quietness in the darkness. Soon you will see the rising sap, the bud, the foliage, the leaf and then the flower. The tiny aconites raise their heads and a thousand voices announce the birth of new life.

"You will be reminded of the old pagans, the uncivilised savages, whose religion was founded on the rituals of nature, who saw in the seasons the divine drama, who constructed from the movements of the stars and the planets the lives of the gods, the powers that watched over them; who paid tribute to the laws which controlled their life, who recognised that the greatest season of all was spring, when birth came upon your world.

"The cycle is repeated in every human life. The pageant of nature is duplicated in every human soul. First there is the spring, with the awakening consciousness; the summer, when man's powers rise to their highest; autumn, when life begins to wane; and winter, when sleep comes to the weary, tired soul. But even after the winter of the physical life, spring comes to the spirit as it awakens in another world to continue that eternal cycle. Take from nature this message, and be assured that the laws which have never failed will continue to operate in your case and in the case of every human life."

At one sitting, one of the circle mentioned the passing of a well-known Spiritualist. "One by one, the Great Harvester gathers them in, so that the course of life may be radiant in a fuller world," commented the guide.

"Tears for your world as they pass beyond your ken; rejoicing in ours as we greet newly-liberated souls who will begin to taste the joys of life indescribable in earthly language," he went on. "I strive always to teach the lesson that death spells freedom, and that whilst you mourn the ones removed from your vibration we rejoice, knowing they have begun a life of new freedom, new happiness, with greater opportunities for expressing that which is within them and which often failed to be realised in the world of matter. You are blessed with the knowledge that they are not lost to you, and I would tell you that just as their power quickens with growth in our life so they always return to you, to help you in the great fight that we are waging.

"That great fight goes on, day by day, in every part of the world of matter—the war between the forces of the spirit and the ugly forces of materialistic selfishness. But we march forward to the inevitable victory, knowing that even if occasionally there are set-backs and it would seem as if the powers of the spirit are vanquished, because of the mighty host ranged with us victory will be ours. You will all look back with great rejoicing at the part you have played in this task, at the comfort and the knowledge you have given to so many. You know not what you do. You know not the countless thousands who, in many places in the world of matter, rejoice because of what we have accomplished.

"You have played your part in spreading this knowledge, which has become a richly-prized treasure to souls who were hungry, waiting for a truth that would bring them satisfaction, that would answer all the aches of their hearts and the questions of their minds and the questings of their souls. Tired with worn-out shibboleths, they turned their faces upwards, waiting for a sign, even as in days gone by men looked to the heavens, waiting for them to reveal that which should come from Beyond. So, with your help, we bring to the world of matter that knowledge which, rightly used, brings freedom to all the children of the Great Spirit—not only freedom to the soul, not only freedom to the mind, but freedom to the body also.

"We are not concerned only with the delivering of souls from bondage. We strive to rescue the bodies of matter from the miserable conditions which are their lot. Ours is a three-fold purpose—freedom for mind, freedom for soul, freedom for body. I know that when, in your work, you tell the world of matter that these are the implications of our truths, you meet with opposition from those who fear that they cannot go all the way. But our truths embrace every aspect of life. Even as there is nothing in the universe beyond the operation of the Great Spirit's law, so there is no facet of life beyond the application of our spiritual truths.

"In all your efforts to uplift the fallen, to give succour to the weak and the helpless, to enable those deprived of the necessities of life to have a share in the plenteous bounty of the Great Spirit, in redressing wrong, in levelling inequalities, in bringing food to hungry people and providing shelter for the homeless, I want you to know that it is all part of the task which belongs to us.

"We do not seek to elevate souls so that they shall be indifferent to the welfare of their fellows. The more knowledge you possess of spiritual truths, the greater must be your desire to serve those less fortunate than yourselves. It matters not by what name you designate those truths. It matters not whether you tie on them the label of politics, economics, religion or philosophy—that is unimportant. What does matter is that our truths should be used to free the world from all its injustices and enable those who have not received their due to obtain their rightful heritage."

"Your body is not you; you are an eternal spirit," said Silver

Birch on another occasion, when he was stressing the value of home circles sitting regularly.

"Though we meet in this manner for but a short time," he added, "it serves to strengthen the bonds that unite us all and enables us to make a stronger contact, for your own spirits condition themselves week after week to the power of the spirit registered and expressed in your midst. Although the physical parts of yourselves are not conscious of the subtle links with the world of spirit, yet your larger selves know in reality. It serves also to remind you—and it is necessary for you to have constant reminders—that you are spiritual and not physical beings. You, who are so accustomed to performing day by day, hour by hour and minute by minute the many physical tasks which are necessary for your material well-being, are apt to forget that the physical is but the outer husk. It is not the inner reality.

"When you see your reflection in the mirror, you are not looking at the individual, but merely the semblance. The physical is but the garment man wears, the means by which he expresses himself in the world of matter. Your body is not you. You are an eternal spirit, part of the life force that sustains the whole universe, part of the Power that fashioned the whole planetary system, that governs the ebb and flow of tides, that regulates the eternal cycle of the seasons, that controls all growth and evolution, that enables the sun to shine and the stars to twinkle. You are divine, just as divine as the Great Spirit, for what you possess that Power possesses. It is the same quality in essence; different in degree but fundamentally the same. And that transcends all material conceptions. It transcends all physical limitations. It is greater than anything you can conceive.

"You are indeed mighty atoms—infinite, yet expressing yourselves in a finite manner. Within you there is a power that one day bursts all its bonds and insists that it shall express itself in a body more fitting to its reality. That you call death, and you mourn and you weep and you sorrow when it happens, because, still thinking that the body is the individual, you believe that death removes the one you love. But death has no power over life; death cannot touch life; death cannot destroy life. The material is not stronger than the spiritual. If the eyes were open, if the ears could hear, if the soul left behind could register the more subtle vibrations of spiritual life, it would see the resurrected spirit, liberated, triumphant, joyous, welcoming the escape from the thraldom and bondage of a material prison.

"Do not grieve for those to whom freedom has come. Do not mourn because the caterpillar has become a beauteous butterfly. Do not weep because the cage has been opened and the bird has been set free. Rejoice, and know that the enfranchised soul has found liberty and that, if you would but unfold the powers that the Great Spirit has given you, you could share some of the new beauty and joy which is theirs. You could understand the plan of death and realise that death is but a stepping-stone, a door through which you enter into the larger freedom of the realms of the spirit.

"I would that I could make you understand. I would that I could make you realise the power that comes to those who rejoice in the liberation that death spells for them. But we are spreading this knowledge; light does come to your world and darkness is dispelled. No longer does mankind trust those who have misled them for centuries. The authority of the churches is vanishing; their power weakens because they refuse to make a place for spiritual truths."

Most people have wondered at one time or another what happens to pet animals after death. Silver Birch was once asked a series of questions on the subject by Sylvia Barbanell, the medium's wife, who was at that time preparing a book on animal survival.

"Do some animals spend their whole time with their human

friends on the Other Side, or is their real home on the animal sphere?" Silver Birch was asked.

"It depends," he replied, "because love is the index. You know that love determines the survival of animals. It is the love that exists between the animal and the person that enables the animal to obtain that temporary consciousness that exists beyond the grave of matter. If an animal and—I do not like the word 'owner,' because no one owns another soul—and the one whom it has served are in the world of spirit together, then the home of the animal is the home of the individual who has always loved it. That is its home. It stays where love is, for love is the link that binds it to the one who loves it. It has no necessity to go to the animal plane.

"Those who dwell in the animal sphere are the ones who come to the world of spirit before the masters, as you call them, arrive in our world, because it is necessary that someone shall take care of them. Otherwise they would be distracted, being cut off from the love which not only warmed their hearts but breathed a temporary immortality into them. Where the animal comes to our world preceding the one who loved it, who gave it shelter and taught it all the habits of memory, of reason, of judgement and affection, it goes to the animal world to await the time when it can greet the one it has missed. There it is put in the charge of those specially trained to look after animals, just as you have trainers in your world to care for animals when their masters and mistresses are away."

"Will you describe what it is that an animal obtains from human contact that makes it survive?" was the next question.

Silver Birch replied: "In the long line of evolution, at some stage the Great Spirit, or the Law, breathed into animal and it became a living soul, conscious, aware of its own existence. Then came the dawn of reason; intelligence bloomed; there was judgement, the ability to reflect, to decide, to weigh and to consider. But potentially all that existed—no matter how far back in the line of evolution you go. It required the breath of the Great Spirit to awaken it. Just as the Great Spirit enabled a divine spark to become a flame, so you, by love, transfer that process to the animal who lives within the shelter of your affection. You are part of the Great Spirit, having the power within you to transfer the attribute of spirit to the next in the line of evolution, so that by your association, by radiating love, you awaken that consciousness which in time, through the process of evolution, would reach its own apex."

"How long does the survival of an animal last?" was another point put. "Is it as long as that of a human being?"

"No," answered Silver Birch, "there is this difference. At some stage the animal and the human evolution inevitably part company. It may take, as you measure time, hundreds of thousands of years, but their rate of spiritual evolution is unequal. The animal has to be left behind because it cannot keep pace with the growing soul that restlessly struggles towards the greater light.

"Once you have passed from the veil of matter and accustomed yourself to conditions of the spiritual life, once you have realised that the ties which bind you to earth are severed, the desire to progress, the desire to unfold the surging divinity within becomes quickened. You seek to unfold all the qualities which, by their practice, will enable you to be of greater service wherever you are. The higher you climb in that realm of spiritual unfoldment, the more difficult is it for the animal to keep pace with you. And so the love which kindled for a while a flame that burned beyond death gradually becomes attenuated. The flame flickers and it merges in the end with the group soul of that species."

"Why are animals, particularly cats and dogs, often more psychic than human beings?" was another topic raised.

"Because although they have not as yet, as far as evolution goes, reached the stage where they become humans," said the spirit sage, "they have not had to face the 'civilised' life that human beings do. If the human had not had the 'benefits' of what you call civilisation, then he would have reached the stage before now where the exercise of psychic qualities was part of his normal life. He has sacrificed that for his civilisation. But the animal, not faced with the economic problems, with the sociological problems that affect human beings, has continued in the evolutionary line to the stage that humans should have reached, but have not, and therefore is in possession of those psychic qualities which humans have, but often repress, because of the material life they have to lead."

Another time, Silver Birch spoke of the spirit world's beauties, saying: "You who are encased in matter, do not yet comprehend beauty as it can be. I have told you before of our light, colour, scenery, trees, birds, rivers, streams, mountains, flowers—and yet your world fears death.

"Death strikes terror into hearts. But you will only begin to live when you are 'dead.' Now you live, but in reality you are almost dead. So many are dead to the things of the Spirit. The little lifeforce flickers in their puny bodies, but no spiritual things can find any response within them.

"But gradually we make progress. Gradually the force of the Spirit increases in strength all over your world of matter. Gradually darkness retreats, as it must when confronted by the light of spiritual truth.

"What a glorious message we have for your world of matter—a message that makes men free and teaches them to rejoice in their divine heritage; a message that teaches them to throw off all shackles and bonds; a message that teaches them to rejoice in the fulness of spiritual knowledge; a message that shows them how to live not only on the planes of matter, but on the planes of Spirit; a message that brings them beauty, love and wisdom, understanding, truth and happiness; a message which speaks of service, service, service.

"And yet we are denied by those who do not understand the revelation of the Great Spirit and who deny the Spirit, as the power of the Spirit has been denied throughout all times.

"I like to remind you of these things, so that you shall remember you are all part of a great spiritual crusade, each of you a soldier, fighting a battle, not with bombs or guns, but with Truth as your weapon, with love in your heart, with a desire to uplift and to serve.

"You have not tasted the joys of the world of spirit. There is nothing in your world of matter with which you can compare the life of the spirit, freed from the trammels of the flesh, with liberty, escaped from the prison of the body of matter, to go where you will, to see your thoughts take shape, to follow out the desires of your heart, to be freed from the troubles of money. No, you have not tasted the joys of the world of spirit."

'Thou art the breath of all life'

"Oh, Great White Spirit, Thou are the breath of life. Thou art the Law that is behind all life. Thou art the centre of all manifestations. Thou art the Spirit that rulest over all things wisely and well. Thou art perfect love and perfect wisdom, and Thou art perfect justice. Thou art perfect law in all its manifestations.

"Thou hast revealed Thyself in the days which have gone by to those whose eyes could pierce the fog of matter and see the vibrations of spirit. Thou hast revealed Thy love to those who can raise themselves up beyond the planes of matter into the realms of spirit.

"Thou hast instructed the wise of ancient days as Thou dost instruct the instruments of our own times, seeking always to reveal the fulness of Thy inspiration, seeking to bring Thy love in manifestation through human hearts, so that the children of matter may know how closely they are bound to Thee.

"Oh, Great Spirit, Thou hast made the whole universe. Thou hast created the greatest of the great. Thou hast created the smallest of the small. And Thou has set in the world of matter the children of earth, giving to each one of them a portion of Thy spirit, so that they can rise superior to all the troubles of earth because of their kinship with Thee.

"Thou has given them the power to share in Thy creation so that they may reveal Thee and help Thee to speed Thy plan in its fulfilment through earth.

"Wherever Thy instruments of earth seek to receive the fulness of Thy love, of Thy wisdom, of Thy power, of Thy purpose, Thou hast sent to them Thy ministers to guard them, to guide them, to inspire them, to lift them up still higher, so that, filled with Thy power, they may help to bring Thy laws into fuller operation.

"We who seek to serve Thee in this temple desire to erect here a place which will enable those who are in despair and bowed down with sorrow to find new hope and new comfort, that those who are tired may find new strength, that those who are weary may find new hope, and that those whose eyes are filled with tears shall find happiness in the knowledge that in Thy kingdom there is no death but only life.

"We would pray, oh, Great Spirit, that all which prevents the fulfilment of Thy love on earth shall be swept away through the co-operation of those who work in the world of matter with those who work from the realm of spirit, always seeking to bring Thee nearer to the children of earth.

"That is the prayer of Thy Indian servant who, with many others, seeks to serve Thee by serving Thy children."

Chapter Three

'A WORLD OF THOUGHT'

W HAT exactly is the spirit world like? Do those who exist in an astral sphere experience a subjective or objective existence? Are there truly "many mansions" to be encountered? What happens to those unfortunates killed, for example, in a bomb explosion?

One sitter confessed to Silver Birch that he found it difficult "to grasp that the astral world is identical with this world."

"The next stage of life to earth is a replica of your world of matter," declared Silver Birch. "Were it not so, the shock for the many who are uninstructed and ignorant would be more than they could stand. And so it has to be accomplished by very easy stages. The next stage of life resembles your world. That is why so many do not know that they have passed beyond the physical. Here essentially it is a world of thought, where thought is reality. And, being a thought world, thought moulds every expression of its life and its activity. Being so near to your world, and peopled by men and women who are naturally still very material in their outlook on life, the expression of their thought is very gross and so whatever they think is in terms of physical things.

"They cannot think of life apart from its physical aspects. There has never filtered into their consciousness any understanding of a life apart from the purely physical. They cannot visualise spiritual activities and, because they cannot visualise them, they have no place in their scheme of things. But there are degrees of astral life, for gradually as awakening comes the grossness slowly disappears and becomes more refined. And life, they begin to see, is something beyond its material aspect. When spiritual realisation dawns they are dead to the astral world and they begin to live in the world of spirit. There are many deaths and many births."

"Are the experiences of people in the astral world subjective or objective?" asked a sitter.

"It is an objective life because life in my world is regulated by people who dwell on that particular plane of expression. As you advance beyond that, you leave it behind. As the spirit qualifies itself, by growth, progress and evolution, so it naturally passes to the next stage of spirit life. It is very objective in its own field of expression."

"So it is not a dream world," the sitter said.

"When they have passed beyond it, it is a dream world," said Silver Birch. "Whilst they are living in it, it is a real world to them. You call them dreams only by comparison. They are not dreams when you are dreaming them. They are dreams when you awaken and, recalling the experience, you say 'That was a dream.' So, when the spirit has passed beyond the lower stages of the astral, it recollects those experiences and says, 'They were dreams.' But when it endured them, they belonged to reality."

"Do we all start our life in the spirit world on this lower astral plane?" a sitter wanted to know.

"Oh, no, it is for the uninstructed and the ignorant," said the guide, "those who are unaware of the existence of spiritual realities, who cannot visualise anything beyond the purely physical. The astral world is part of the world of spirit. It is one life in many varying grades, from the lower reaches to the highest stages. It is not divided into watertight compartments. We have to give you terms that you can understand."

Telling about growth in the spirit world, Silver Birch explained: "You do not climb from one sphere into another; you grow, you evolve. The lower gives way to the higher. You 'die' and are born again and again. You do not lose the astral body in quite the same way that you lose the material body. It becomes more rarefied, it becomes refined, as the lower drops away. That is its death, for death really means transformation, resurrection, the rising of the higher out of the lower. Whenever we try to explain our world of spirit, which is freed from the limitations of your world, with its restrictions of time and space, we always have difficulty. The lower cannot grasp the higher, the finite cannot include the infinite, the lesser cannot hold the greater, but only by striving can you increase your capacity to understand."

"In the astral world, does one retain such things as the heart and pulse beats?" asked a sitter at another séance.

"Whether they retain these organs depends on their state of consciousness," said Silver Birch. "If they are completely ignorant of a life after yours and they do not think that there is another world, then they have a complete replica of everything they had in the physical world, and they continue every bodily function in all its details—*every* function."

"And what happens at the passing of someone who understands about the spirit world?" asked the sitter.

"The astral body goes through a process of rarification," the spirit replied. "As you appreciate that there is no need for certain organs, you gradually find they become atrophied and in the end they disappear."

"Does that happen immediately after passing, or is it a gradual process?" a circle member asked.

"It depends on the state of your consciousness," said the guide. "The higher your consciousness, the less the need for adjustment. You must always remember that ours is a mind world, a spirit world where consciousness is king. The mind is enthroned and mind rules. What mind dictates is reality. When you have read of the appearance of those who come from the higher, or inner, planes, do you not find they are described as shining figures radiating light, rather than as having shape? That is because personality has gone. It is because there is less of the bodily expression about them."

"What shape are the higher intelligences?" asked a sitter. "What shape is beauty?" countered the guide. "What shape is love? What shape is light?"

"Does colour form the basis of recognition when you get beyond shape?" asked another sitter.

"Yes," said the guide, "but whereas you are governed by certain primary colours we have other ranges of colour beyond your comprehension. We can identify some of the higher teachers by the radiance of their appearance, by the light that comes with the message; because often there is no form of any kind. There is a thought, accompanied by radiance."

Then a sitter asked about the popular idea of angels with wings. How did the wings originate?

"When, in the days of long ago, they used to think of the universe," said the guide, "they divided it into three distinct compartments—there was the earth on which they stood, there was hell which was underneath them, and there was heaven which was above them. They knew there were visitors from both places, and they could only visualise people coming from heaven as having wings. They could not understand how people coming from a long distance above could reach them, unless, like the birds, they had wings. That is how the idea of angels with wings was born."

"Are there beings with wings?" asked another sitter.

"Yes," said the guide. "But it is only a thought form, for we require no wings in our world. It is a picture. Often we can only convey ideas to our instruments by building pictures, and the picture of a being with wings enfolding someone suggests guardianship. But there are some who, having to care for the children, have, as it were, grown these wings because there are always children who expect to see them."

The closeness of those on the Other Side was stressed when Silver Birch mentioned many dead friends and relatives of the sitters who had asked him to convey messages.

"Try to remember that all of them are real human beings," he said, "who are just as interested in you as ever they were before. Though they do not speak to you, and you cannot hear them, they are here, each striving to do the utmost to assist you. They are closer than you know. They know your secrets, the unspoken desires of your minds, your wishes, your hopes and your fears. And all the while they bring their influence to bear on you, to guide you so that you may be able to extract from your earthly lives the experiences so necessary for the growth of your souls. They are not vague, shadowy, nebulous beings, but real men and women who love you still and who are in reality closer to you than ever they have been before."

"What class of spirit beings would be helped by spiritual healing?" one of the circle queried.

"Those whose spiritual bodies have suffered shock," replied the guide. "Those who require the power that will enable adjustments to be made, so that they are ready for the spiritual life. Those whose brains were imperfect registers for their minds, all those where the spiritual body never received the fulness of expression because of some defect."

Sometimes people wonder what happens to those killed suddenly, as by a bomb explosion. One night Silver Birch was asked what arrangements were made in the spirit world for receiving people who passed on as the result of bombing.

"This requires simply an extension of the normal facilities which are in operation all the time to deal with arrivals in our world," came the answer. "Just as you, in time of war, have to prepare hospitals and institutions to care for the wounded, thus extending the service that is given to those who fall by the wayside in more normal times, so do we have to add to our arrangements to care for the many souls, some sick, some unready, and too many unprepared, so as to assist them and help them to understand the new life into which they have been plunged."

Another interesting sidelight on life in the Beyond was given when the guide repeated to a sitter a message from a spirit individual who wished to apologise for trouble he had caused during his life on earth.

"I know it does not matter to you, now," said Silver Birch, "but he had to voice his regret. I did not say it so much for you, but because it helps him. When they make these requests it is a sign that they are finding their true selves, and that is why I conveyed the message. I know that to you it is past and forgotten. But it is registered and cannot be obliterated until growth takes place and recognition is made."

Once Silver Birch asked those present: "Have you ever considered the feelings of those who return to you from my world and who cannot bring their influence to bear upon you? Have you considered the many who pass from your world into mine and then, because their focus changes and they see life for the first time in its proper perspective, they eagerly return to bring their tidings of joy to the ones they love?

"But your world is dead to them," he went on. "It cannot hear and it cannot see. Many foolishly imagine that their five senses are the sum total of all reality and naught exists beyond these crude and clumsy senses.

"Often we see the return from our world of eager souls, yearning to make their presence felt, trying to touch with outstretched hands the ones they have left behind for a while. We see dismay written on their faces as they learn with regretful surprise that no longer can they make an impression on your world. They cannot be heard; they cannot be seen; they cannot be felt, with all the will in the world, even in those homes where love reigns. And, very disconsolately, we have to tell them that, until the ones they seek to touch can be brought within the radius of spirit influence, it is hopeless to try to reach them."

Then Silver Birch told of another aspect of the failure of those in the spirit world to reach us.

"I have accompanied many whom you call pillars of the Church," he said. "They have gone back to their places of worship, to their cathedrals and churches. They have listened to the recital of much that they now know is false, and their hearts have been filled with heaviness and their heads have been bowed down in sorrow as they realised that they too had helped to perpetuate a system of error and superstition."

"That must be hell for them," commented a sitter.

"It is purgatory," replied the guide. "Yet it is the Law, for each must undo the wrong that he has done. Each must pay the price for the life he has lived. In eternal justice, all accounts are settled with equity, and none escapes the operation of the Law."

"How could such a man undo the wrong he has done?" asked one of the circle.—"He has to meet every one to whom he has given wrong teaching, and undo all his error."

"Does he have to meet face to face everyone to whom he has preached?"—"Yes."

"But, in the meantime, they may have been put right," said the sitter.—"If that is done, his task is lightened."

"Suppose he thought he was doing the right thing—does that affect it?"—"Yes, that helps, because motive always counts."

"But if he thought he was doing the right thing, would he still have to meet them all?" persisted the questioner.

"Not if he thought so in his soul," replied the guide. "But there are many who do not think so in their souls, to whom pride and arrogance, possessions and wealth are more important than what is the truth. When you have become part of a system, when you are enmeshed in it, then it holds you in its chains. You seek to paralyse your reason by repeating old shibboleths.

"Our quarrel is not with the honest man who makes mistakes without realising it, but with those who know within their hearts that their allegiance is not to truth but to a system which they seek to perpetuate—or else they are afraid of facing the future if they discard what has come to them from the past. We do not condemn the honest men who do wrong because they do not realise it, but we condemn the many who know that what they say and do is wrong, who employ casuistry and who justify themselves by saying, 'If we do not do this, we have no guidance, we have no teaching to offer.'

"But even where wrong is done unintentionally, it must be put right. Then it is not so much a purgatory as a delight. It is a joy of service because it is done with willingness of soul."

One sitter recalled that he was at one time a Methodist missionary. "Do you mean I shall have to put right the wrong teaching I gave to all the people to whom I preached?" he asked.

"Yes, if they have not found truth by then, if because of what you have said you have delayed a soul in reaching the light you will have to help him to find the light," was the guide's reply.

"That sounds rather overwhelming, for I have spoken to so many people," said the sitter.

"You, like all others, will have to face all your tasks," said Silver Birch. "But you need not worry."

"Probably those he has helped since he gave up his ministry will help him to bring the light to the others," suggested another sitter.

"Yes," replied the guide. "Eternal justice is not mocked. I wish that you could see the operation of Law as I see it and know how finely balanced are the scales of justice. Then you would know that the Great Spirit makes no mistakes.

"Do you not realise that every teacher has a grave responsibility? You hear me say to you so often, 'You have knowledge; but you have the responsibility that comes with knowledge.' If you seek to lift yourself up above your fellows, to guide and instruct them, you must be sure of the ground on which you stand. If you have not subjected yourself to every search, to every test, if you have not faced all possible criticism, if you are content to be indifferent, to give a teaching without knowing for certain that your words are true, you must pay the price for your sloth and your carelessness."

The effect that wrong teaching can have on a soul was illustrated at another sitting. One of the circle told Silver Birch of the experience of some Spiritualists who had been able to help a number of spirit beings who said they had been living in the cemeteries, waiting with their bodies for the Judgement Day. He asked whether such a thing was possible.

"It is quite true," replied the guide. "That is one of our great troubles. They expect these things and nothing can be done with them until they learn to change their thoughts. For practically their whole earthly lives they have moulded the thought form that, when the body dies, they will wait until the Angel Gabriel sounds his trumpet. And until they can destroy, with adjustment, the power that they have created it holds them in that prison.

"It is just the same as those who refuse to believe that they have passed on. As long as they refuse to believe it, we cannot make them believe it. You have no idea of the difficulties when we try to convince them that they are dead. I remember a long argument I had with a man who was a Christadelphian. He looked at me and said, 'How can I be dead if I am alive?' He would not believe me and said he would wait for the Resurrection—and he stayed there."

"What do they do with their time?" asked a sitter.

"They wait," said the guide. "You must remember that there is no such thing as time to us. If they knew that they were waiting, that would destroy the thought-form. It is a self-made prison. But it is so hard to convey these things to you. We have no time as you understand it, because we have no earth spinning round on its axis, dependent on the sun to give night and day. How would you count yesterday and to-morrow if there were no divisions of night and day?"

"But even if there were no divisions of time, we would be conscious of time passing," said one present.

"No, you would be conscious of growth and evolution in relation to events which pass around you," corrected the guide. "But time is not passing. Your spirit is growing and events are taking place around you. Time is merely your measurement of your relationship to events. If you are unconscious there is no time, because your relationship to events has altered. When you dream, your relationship to events is altered and so things happen more quickly than they do when you are chained to your earthly body."

'Thou hast reigned supreme'

"Oh, Great White Spirit, Thy laws uphold all the universe. Thou art responsible for all life, for Thou hast created it. Thou hast endowed the children of matter with Thine own divinity.

"Thou hast made them like Thee and placed within their souls the power which unites them with Thee throughout all infinity, so that as they evolve they can become more like Thee.

"Oh, Great White Spirit, Thou hast reigned supreme throughout all the ages of time and Thou wilt reign supreme throughout all the ages yet to come, for Thou art the Great Spirit of all life.

"Thou dost sustain all things and Thou art manifested in every phase of life, whether it is revealed to the consciousness of those in the world of matter or whether it registers far beyond in the planes of spirit.

"Thou hast called us to Thy service so that we, who are Thy messengers, can work to bring Thy will into fruition and can help to reveal Thy plan and make it manifest on earth.

"We would co-operate with the children of matter so that they may understand Thee and understand themselves, so that they may replace their systems of hate with love, their selfishness with service, so that they may abolish war and have peace, so that they may abolish starvation and have the plenty which Thou has showered into the world.

"Oh, Great Spirit, we thank Thee for those hours which we spend together with Thy children who dwell in the lower planes of life, for out of their co-operation we shall be enabled to achieve greater things for Thee, to bring succour to the distressed, light to those in darkness, strength to the weak, healing to the sick, peace to those who are in the storms of life.

"We thank Thee for this haven of refuge, for this temple of light, and we work to enable all the obstacles that prevent the free communion with the world of spirit to be surmounted, so that Thy will shall reign supreme.

"For this we pray and labour, so that we might serve Thee by serving Thy children. This is the prayer of Thy Indian servant."

Chapter Four

'A WILLING SURRENDER'

"NOW concerning spiritual gifts, brethren, I would not have you ignorant . . . there are diversities of gifts, but the same Spirit . . . to one is given . . . the gifts of healing . . . to another the discerning of spirits." Well, despite this Biblical statement there is a good amount of ignorance about mediumship.

So it was that the part played in trance communication by the medium's mind was explained by Silver Birch on one occasion. It began with his comment that he had a little difficulty in controlling because the medium was falling asleep. "That is no good for me," he said.

"Why is that?" asked a sitter.

"I must have control over all that regulates the body," replied Silver Birch.

"Could you not have control if the medium was asleep?" the sitter asked.

"No," said the guide. "Because I must use his subconscious mind to direct his body, and it becomes quiescent in sleep. Trance is not the same as sleep."

"But does not the medium go outside of his body in both cases?" the sitter added.

"No, it is not a question of the medium being inside or outside," replied the guide. "You are dealing with consciousness and its functioning, and that is not in or out."

"I thought the medium's consciousness stood aside," was the circle member's comment.

"Yes, but that is a temporary separation from his physical body," said Silver Birch. "It is a willing surrender, instead of the negation which sleep is. All mediumship is conscious co-operation between our world and yours. There are examples of unconscious co-operation when the faculties are stimulated for a time, but where there is a real work to be done between a guide and an instrument, the co-operation must be a conscious one, a willingness on the part of the medium to take part in all the machinery associated with the development of mediumship."

"Haven't there been cases where the medium has been used in his sleep and trance messages have come through him?" the guide was asked.

"There might have been," he said, "but it is a reversal of the process which should normally be used."

"It is possible that the medium agreed in his sleep to be so used," remarked the sitter.

"Yes, but as you know, we always defer to the wishes of the instrument," said Silver Birch, "unless they are unimportant, and then we suggest what should be done. But of course this body does not belong to us; it belongs to the tenant who inhabits it. If he cares to surrender the lease to us for a little while, that is well and good, but to rob him of his tenancy without his permission is contrary to the Law. It is a natural surrender, with a respect on both sides for the forces which will inhabit the body."

Asked to tell the circle something about the employment of the subconscious mind in trance communication, Silver Birch said:

"There is much misconception about it. Very briefly, mind has many functions. Man is an expression of consciousness, and consciousness is the all-important thing. Consciousness is individual life; individual life is consciousness. Wherever there is consciousness there is individual spirit; and wherever there is individual spirit there is consciousness. You are not aware of the fulness of your consciousness in the physical world in which you live because your consciousness is much larger—to use a term that you will understand—than the physical body through which it is trying to express itself. The smaller cannot contain the larger; the lesser cannot hold the greater.

"And so throughout all your earthly life you express but a mere fraction of that larger consciousness which you will come to recognise in the days after you have passed through the gate of death. Even then you will not immediately become aware of all your consciousness, for it is only through evolution, even in our world, that more and more of the consciousness can be registered through its vehicle.

"Your mind, which is the director of your intelligence, the controller of all your individual life, does not function actively and consciously for every requirement of your physical body. So many of the functions which are necessary for your life in this world are automatic and mechanical. Once the consciousness has arranged the muscles or the nerves, or the cells, or the tissues, and their co-ordination necessary to perform that task, it relegates their repetition to the subconscious part of your mind.

"For example, when you eat you automatically open your mouth, which means the interplay of many nerves and forces before the jaws can move. Nervous impulses have to be sent from the brain, which is the physical counterpart of the mind, and then your teeth have to open and similar instructions have to be given by the brain. All that is automatic. You do not, every time you pick up a morsel of food, deliberately go through all the processes necessary before you can eat. You do them automatically; the subconscious mind does them for you. When you were a baby you had to learn them all one by one; now it is done unthinkingly; purely mechanically.

"You will find that most of the control, therefore, of your bodily—and, to a large extent, your mental—functions have been relegated to the subconscious mind, which is a department, the basement, of your conscious mind. You read a book and you stop and ask yourself what you think of it, and the reply automatically is flashed into your mind. It is your subconscious mind which registers the answer for you, having learned through association with your consciousness the reason that you employ. You hear a speech and if at any time you are asked, 'What do you think of it?' even unthinkingly you provide the answer.

"When, however, you are confronted with problems outside of your ordinary experience, which have not been performed or solved before by the subconscious mind, then your consciousness has to start work, because a new track is involved. But, with these exceptions, where you have to employ original thinking —if such a phrase can be used in that connection—most of your life is relegated to your subconscious mind. It acts as storekeeper; it takes charge of all the records of your memory; it controls most of your living processes; and therefore, from many aspects, it is the most important part of you.

"When it comes to mediumship, it stands to reason, does it not, that where an intelligence which is foreign to the intelligence which has expressed itself through the bodily organism has to function, it is easier for it to take control of the subconscious mind, which is already accustomed to acting on the directions from the conscious mind. It is used to taking orders; it is used to having tasks assigned to it and performing them without interruption, save if anything goes wrong.

"Nearly all forms of mediumship involve the use of the subconscious mind of the medium, for that is the secret of his personality. There, embedded in its storehouse, are all the facets of his individuality. In trance mediumship, what the guide has first of all to learn to avoid is that in controlling his instrument he so takes charge that he does not get from the instrument the usual automatic responses that the medium does, when his consciousness calls on his subconsciousness. That is the whole keynote."

"Has he to still the subconscious mind?" asked a sitter.

"No," said Silver Birch. "The guide has to harmonise his personality with the medium's to achieve such a perfect blending that he superimposes his own thought through being in co-operation. At the same time he has to be master of that subconsciousness which, the moment it gets the association of another directing intelligence, begins to send up impulses, just as when you depress the keys of a typewriter letters move up. That is what the guide has to learn, to avoid that happening.

"You can conceive that, as you are dealing with a living being, with an individual with ideas of his own, with prejudices, likes and dislikes, you are bound in all forms of control to get some aspects of the medium. It is impossible, as I have told you, ever entirely to eliminate the medium. The degree of elimination is dependent on the success in blending the guide's personality with that of his instrument. If it were possible to effect a perfect fusion, then there would be no subconscious interference by the subconscious.

"It is not that you eliminate the medium—you cannot do that—but you have to blend. That is what development of mediumship is. That is why you sit in circles. That is why you have séances, so that the power that is gathered from all those who assemble is used to aid the blending. That is why harmony is essential. That is why, if there is friction among sitters, it is impossible to get harmony between the guide, and the medium. You are dealing with mental forces all the time and, though there is nothing visible to show, all the unseen thoughts, impulses, wills, desires, wishes of all the sitters have an effect on the communications that take place. The more proficient the guide, the more experienced, the greater the state of harmony between him and his instrument, the less will be the subconscious interference."

"Is it better, from your point of view, to choose a medium

whose desires and feelings are more or less the same as those of the guide?" was one aspect raised.

"It all depends," replied the spirit sage. "That is one of the debatable subjects, and there is difference of opinion even in our world. You must remember that we are human beings, and we do not agree on every detail in the processes involved in communication.

"There are some who say that more success is achieved by using an ignorant medium, one who knows so little that his subconsciousness can present no barrier. To that, others reply that his mere ignorance is a barrier because it creates a wall which has to be broken down. The same school argues that where you have a well-filled mind you have a better instrument on which to play, for greater music is possible from an instrument created by craftsmanship than a cheap instrument that you purchase for a few pence in your world, that the better the instrument the better the results our world can get from it. I incline to that belief."

"Why should a medium with more knowledge be better than an ignorant one?" asked a sitter. "Is it not a question of character as well?"

"I am talking about trance mediumship," replied the guide. "Character is a separate issue which involves other factors. I am referring to the actual processes, or, if you like to use the word, the mechanics of communication. I will put it in a very simple way. A violinist will obtain better results from a Strad than he will from a cheap fiddle because the beauty and quality of that instrument enable him to produce better results. The other is a limitation to him.

"The character of the medium has a great effect on the quality of the communicator who can register through him, and, in physical manifestations, on the quality of the results obtained. The lower the character—and I am using these words only in terms of comparison—of the physical medium, the poorer, for example, is the ectoplasm that is used, not poorer physically but from a spiritual point of view. Character determines the quality of the power of attraction between the spirit and the medium. It would be impossible, for example, for the ones you recognise as saints, because of their high spiritual status, to manifest through a medium of very low character, because there is no point of contact."

"With physical mediumship the subconscious mind also seems to have an effect," remarked a sitter. "Can you explain that?"

"The focal point of every séance is the medium," said Silver Birch. "You are not using a telephone, you are not using a telegraph pole, you are not using a morse key. You are using a living instrument, and the qualities of his life impregnate the communications.

"It is well that it is so. If it were possible, which it is not, to reduce all communication between these two states of life to a purely mechanical apparatus, I know that most of the beauty and sacredness would be lost. At every séance the medium is the focal point. You cannot eliminate him. It is all his qualities that are being used. Even when a trumpet is raised or a materialisation is formed, the foundation comes from the medium, and whatever qualities the medium possesses, in some form or another they are conveyed in the results of the séance."

"Why is it that the heart and pulse beats alter when a spirit communicator takes control?" the guide was asked at another sitting. "Are they, as a rule, the heart and pulse beats of the spirit?"

"When spirits are controlling the medium," Silver Birch replied, "they are registering through the subconscious mind and automatically their consciousness regulates the primary functions of the body, which are the beat of the heart and the pulse, the temperature and the circulation of the blood. That is why you notice a change of breathing when control is being effected. It is the transitory stage. But what happens is that the guide is reproducing, by association with matter, his own personality as it was expressed in a body. For example, I use a Red Indian body and thus, through the medium, the pulse beat is that of the Red Indian body, because it is easier to take all that consciousness belonging to the astral body and transfer it rather than to start from the beginning."

"So the medium's pulse now is different than it was half an hour ago," remarked a sitter. "Yes," replied the guide.

Then a sitter recalled an experiment in which changes were observed when a little boy was controlling a medium, and asked whether it would be done consciously or automatically in that case.

"It would be natural in that case," said the guide.

"It would not be done for him by the guide, would it?" asked a sitter.

"It would not be necessary," said Silver Birch. "The subconscious mind of the medium would be ready. The child would be pushed in, and automatically it would register its own childlike vibrations through the subconscious mind and so the pulse and the heart would beat accordingly."

"Does that depend on the development of the control or of the medium?" was the next question.

"It depends on the relationship that exists between the two," said the guide. "I can control this instrument and leave his pulse beat either normal or abnormal."

Another sitter recalled experiments where the alteration was apparently simulated artificially, as when the control made the pulse in one wrist stop beating while that in the other continued. "Yes, it can be done artificially," said Silver Birch. "But you could do all these things yourself. The yogi learns how to make his mind control all the nerve centres. It is all a question of concentration and practice."

'To abolish distress and suffering'

"Oh, Great White Spirit, Thou art the source and centre of all life. Thou art the ruler of all life, for Thou art in all life and Thy laws sustain and control all life throughout Thy wondrous universe in all its infinite manifestations.

"Thy laws reign supreme and Thou knowest all that happens, whether it be the mightiest of the mighty or the smallest of the small, for all things are controlled by Thy laws and Thy laws work through all.

"Oh, Great Spirit, Thou hast placed Thyself within the children of matter so that they are united with Thee and so that they can become more like Thee through evolution and unfoldment. Thou hast placed Thy children in the world of matter with opportunities of serving Thee by expressing Thee and enabling Thy laws to work through them.

"Thou hast given them free will and Thou hast given them the power to discern between that which is right and that which is wrong. Thou hast given them, in Thy spirit, the power to shape the world in which they live so that it can become a kingdom of heaven.

"Oh, Great White Spirit, Lord of all life throughout all ages, Thou rulest with wisdom and justice, with mercy but, more than all these things, with love.

"Thou hast sent Thy ministers to tend, to watch, to inspire and to co-operate with all willing souls who seek to abolish distress and suffering, illness, sickness, disease, crime, war, and all that brings darkness where there should be light, all that makes suffering where there should be peace, and all that makes starvation where there should be plenty.

"Oh, Great Spirit, we seek to work with those who would establish Thy kingdom on earth, to free men from the prisons that they have erected for themselves, so that, instead of stooping under the loads that they have placed on their own backs, they may free themselves from their self-imposed bondage and, gazing towards Thy sun, allow its rays to illumine them so that they may work in the light instead of the dark.

"To that end we pray and work, seeking to serve Thee by serving Thy children."

Chapter Five

'THE POWER OF THE SPIRIT'

EVEN the most optimistic among us sometimes has jaded off days when just nothing seems to go right. Calamity follows calamity, annoyance follows annoyance. Yet truth to tell so often are these just minor irritations which, when viewed with a long-term perspective, pale into their rightful place.

Silver Birch always stressed the need—and note—of optimism. This time he pointed out just how much psychic truth had advanced despite opposition from Orthodoxy and other vested interests.

"When our work was started, men despised us," he said, reviewing almost a century of psychic progress. "The finger of scorn was pointed at our puny efforts. 'Table-rappers' they sneered and jeered. But it was all part of a Plan, a mighty Purpose. Slowly our influence grew and spread. We brought within the radius of our influence those who in your world commanded respect for distinguished service in their walks of life. We chose them because we knew that their testimony would be respected by all except those whose eyes were blinded by prejudice and whose reason was clouded by superstition.

"More and more were brought within the radius of spirit influence. The power of the spirit descended on more and more instruments. The circle widened and spread. Gradually we brought together men of science, of medicine, of philosophy, of religion—from every activity in the world of matter, so that all could pay their tribute to facts which denied the false materialism which had become fashionable, facts which pointed the way to a new and higher conception of life, facts which spelled death to materialism. And in a short time, a very short time, the despised 'table-rappers' have become the only movement in the world which can save religion from decay.

"See in that the lesson of what has been accomplished in less than a hundred years, and realise what will be accomplished in the days that lie before us. But the great message to-day is: we want more instruments and we want instruments who will have perfect faith in the power of the spirit to guide and inspire them. We want all those who have this knowledge to use it, so that others may benefit, so that the truth may bring light into darkened lives.

"We want this truth so applied to daily life that all men may recognise its messengers by virtue of the life that they live and see that they are indeed divine messengers because of the probity and uprightness of their own characters. And then we want them all to go out into the world and to apply that knowledge to every facet of human life. We want them first to improve themselves and, having done that, to fit themselves for the task of giving service to others. More has been accomplished than you can see, but that is naught compared with what will be done in the days that lie before us.

"Look around your world. Read the signs. See the collapse of all old-fashioned, out-worn creeds and dogmas, and see how in your own times the fabric of theology is being destroyed. The structure built on a foundation of false faith is collapsing all around you. We have built on a foundation of knowledge, and there is no storm that can arise that will ever shake the foundations we have built on, for it is on truth, divine truth. Long after you have ceased to register in the world of matter the temple you helped to erect will stand secure, a monument to your labours."

On another occasion, making the same point, Silver Birch declared:

"Truth marches forward; the forces that belong to darkness,

ignorance, superstition and confusion are in retreat. Victory is on the side of the power of the spirit as its forces gather strength, breaking through in places hitherto considered impossible. That is the great message we repeat and repeat, for you are all labouring for this new order of being. The transformation takes place now very slowly. As the old gives place to the new, many upheavals will occur. They are all part of the Plan.

"I urge you always to remember the fundamental spiritual truths. Cling to them and build on them your religion, your science, your philosophy, your ethics, your morality. Discard all the fanciful trappings that come to those whose imaginations desire high-sounding philosophies. Ours is but the simple truth which in its utter simplicity can be appreciated and understood by all, for we strive to reveal the children of the Great Spirit as they are—part of the Great Spirit, truly the children of God, all bound together by the infinite eternal tie of spirit, all part of a vast spiritual family, all equal in the sight of the Great Spirit.

"Those who see with the eyes of the spirit see beyond the confines of barriers of race, nationality, clime, colour and creed and discern that tie of the spirit that binds together all humanity as one. It is very necessary to remind your world of these simple truths. For too long have they floundered in creeds and dogmas, ceremonies and rituals which have nothing whatever to do with religion or the Great Spirit of life.

"We care not for creed, doctrine or dogma—unless they enable a soul to live a better life. We are not concerned with aught but action, for it is the living of your daily lives that is of fundamental importance. No creed, no dogma and no ritual can alter by one hair's breadth the sequence of the law of cause and effect; neither can they detract one iota or add a particle to your spiritual state, which is determined only by your daily lives. Our allegiance is always to the Great Spirit of life and to His eternal natural laws, not to a church, not to a book, not to a creed.

"Rejoice that an impetus has been given to the power of the spirit to manifest. See the new instruments who have been brought within the radius of spirit power. See the new lines of communication that have been made. Witness the breaking down of vested interests and obstacles that have stood in the way of progress. We are part of a victorious army who fight not with swords, not with guns, but with love in our hearts, with tolerance, with charity, with the desire to serve. Our weapons are truth and reason. We desire only to bring a richness and a greater beauty into the lives of those who are denied their rightful heritage.

"We make war on all those forces that stand between the Great Spirit and His children, wherever they may be, whoever they may be, and we yield to none in our determination to quicken wherever we can the advancement of the Kingdom of Heaven on earth. We have faced the opposition of lies, calumnies, hostility and persecution, and because valiant hearts and determined souls have stood for truth the power of the spirit has been enabled to manifest. Today there are many soldiers standing at the outposts of the New World. I urge you to be of good cheer. Let not your hearts be troubled. See behind all the changing events the unfolding of the plans of the Great Spirit, and know that you are helping to build the New World, for truth is marching forward all the time.

"Tell the people not to be depressed or sad, for they are beginning to reap the harvest of the labours of pioneers of the past, and they are preparing the way for greater liberty and greater freedom for the children of to-morrow. Fear belongs to the darkness of men's ignorance. Strength comes with confidence, in the knowledge that the storms of life cannot upset or overwhelm the soul who knows that he is the Great Spirit.

"I have a few simple truths to teach, simple but important,

for it is in the application of these truths that the world is saved from itself and the Great Spirit is enabled to be made manifest. Go forward always in the knowledge that you indeed have a priceless gift of spiritual truth, which banishes all the fogs and mists and enables you to pierce the gloom with the light of understanding. But remember always the responsibility that comes with knowledge, for once you know you are not the same as when you were ignorant. He who denies the power of the spirit when he knows commits a greater sin than the one who in ignorance opposes spiritual truth.

"Use your knowledge wisely and well. Strive always to bring others within the radius, to touch their souls and reach their hearts, for we are always seeking to banish the tears of sorrow, to remove the ache from the leaden heart, the blinkers that prevent the eyes from seeing the radiant spirit truths. We strive to bring the Great Spirit nearer to His children and His children nearer to the Great Spirit of all life, to bring into operation those laws that belong to the higher phases of life, so that in their manifestation selfishness may disappear and the fulness of life be the joy of all who dwell in your world."

When one member of the circle tried to compare the progress of psychic knowledge with the initial growth of other religions, Silver Birch suggested that such a comparison should not be made.

"We have made progress," he said, "but then you must remember that we do not think of Spiritualism as being comparable with other religions. To us, it is the natural law of the universe; it is not a teaching which is to be crystallised and made into a fixed number of articles of acceptance. Christianity was but one means of expression of the natural law; so was Judaism, so was Buddhism, so was every other religion that your world has ever had. To each inspired leader there came the vision, the inspiration, the understanding of natural law, to be dispensed according to the growth, development, evolution, customs, training and understanding of the day in which he lived. As the seer received it, he transmitted it to those who were receptive. It was a portion of truth. Alas, that portion became overlaid.

"The simple truth could not stay in all its pristine beauty. It became a mixture of inspiration to which were added the current beliefs, the theological conceptions, religious practices, inherited traditions. In time that which was of the Great Spirit was completely submerged, and so a new need arose to resurrect and resuscitate that which man had buried. All the religions of the past—there are no exceptions—are part and parcel of that same inspiration which is reaching your world today. It is hard to compare one with another because they are aspects of one truth. Circumstances are different. You have today means of communication which were not available in days gone by. You do not have difficulties of transmission. You can reach one another, you can send messages to one another, you can encircle the globe in the fraction of a minute.

"What is true is that there was launched from my world an organised effort according to a plan well conceived in all its details. It was determined that this time spiritual truth had come to stay and no power on earth would prevent it. The plan is succeeding, for now the knowledge of spiritual realities is making itself felt in all the countries of your world, and wherever instruments are raised up there the power of the spirit flows through them and another outpost has been established.

"You know that always I have insisted on the necessity for more and more instruments. That is the great need, so that there can be more channels through whom our knowledge, our teaching, our love, our comfort, our guidance can be given to your world. Every new instrument is another nail in the coffin of materialism. Every new instrument is a victory for the Great Spirit and spiritual truth. That is why mediums are important—because they are mediums. That is why I rejoice that I have found an instrument through whom I can be used to give whatever comes to me from the realms of knowledge, light and wisdom."

'The centre of all life'

"Let us pray to the Great Spirit. Oh, Great White Spirit, the whole of life revolves around Thee, and Thou dost hold in the embrace of Thy love the whole of humanity, whether it expresses itself in the world of matter or in the world of spirit.

"Oh, Great White Spirit, Thou art the centre of all life, for Thy Being is expressed in all life. Thy spirit giveth life and Thou art life itself, for with Thee there is life, and without Thee, there is naught.

"Oh, Great White Spirit, Thy love sustains all things. Thy wisdom has created all things and Thy purpose shapes all things. Thy plan gradually comes into fulfilment as it expresses itself throughout all the spheres of existence.

"Thou art the Great Spirit, Who art so great that no mind, however exalted, can understand Thy fulness. Thou art the Great Spirit, and yet Thou art within the smallest of the small as Thou art expressed in the greatest of the great.

"Nothing happens in the whole universe that Thou dost not know, for Thy laws embrace all life and Thou, Great Spirit, art everywhere, for Thy spirit pervadeth all things.

"And we, who are Thy servants and who seek to express Thy laws, ask of Thee for that power which will enable us to work in co-operation with all willing souls in the world of matter, that we can build stronger bridges between the plane of matter and the plane of spirit, over which many more messengers can return, bringing Thy message of love and good will and peace to the world of matter.

"Over these bridges may there return not only Thy

messengers but also those who belong to those still in the world of matter.

"We ask at this time, when all thoughts are centred on the one who came to earth to demonstrate Thy love and Thy power, that the children of earth shall remember that within them is Thy power, which will enable them to sweep away all the obstacles that prevent peace in their world. If they would but reveal Thee in their lives and in their actions, then Thy will would be done.

"This is the prayer of Thy Indian servant who seeks to serve."

Chapter Six

'THE LIGHT OF TRUTH'

TWO thousand years ago there died upon a cross a man whose influence over world events and many mortal minds still reigns supreme. But what has Jesus done since then? Silver Birch once explained that Jesus was in charge of a drive from the spirit world to give to this earth once more the essentials of Christianity, which had become overgrown with creeds and dogmas and vested interests. Then, at another sitting, Silver Birch spoke of him again, declaring:

"Yesterday the Nazarene was crucified, only because the priests hated him, because the power of the spirit was made manifest through him, because he was of God, because it meant the shattering of their vested interest. Today there is still the same opposition. They have tried to crucify Truth, but they cannot. Truth survives all the opposition, all the hostility, because it is Truth. While outside the Churches the power of the spirit is being made manifest, these empty desolate mausoleums have no light of the spirit to relieve their gloomy darkness."

"Do you think we should be better off if the Church were to die tomorrow?" asked a sitter.

"I have no interest in churches, bricks and mortar, altars and steeples," replied the guide. "They make no appeal to me. I am not interested in buildings. I am interested in souls, and I strive to drive away all the barriers between the Great Spirit and His children. Unfortunately, the Churches stand in the way. What a condemnation that is! The Great Spirit is not restricted to a church. The Great Spirit is not captured in a building. His power is to be seen when human life reveals itself in all its radiant divinity, in the desire to give selfless service, and reveals itself by devotion to suffering, helpless humanity. That is where we find the Great Spirit.

"Here and there, it is true, there are individuals in the Churches who strive to do their best. It is the system that I condemn, because it stands in the way and must be swept on one side. Religion has naught to do with ritual and ceremony, with beautiful singing and chanting, with jewels and gorgeous raiments and vestments. Religion is service, serving the Great Spirit by serving His children. How often have I said that! Your churches have divided mankind, separated nations and classes, caused war and bitterness, rancour, bloodshed, torture, inquisition. They have opposed the march of knowledge, invention, science, discovery. They have sought to protect a vested interest, fearful and afraid lest the new knowledge should engulf them. The truth is here to stay. It cannot be stemmed any longer."

A sitter remarked that the Nazarene must feel very strongly about those things.

"Misrepresented, worshipped, deified—where do you think the Nazarene is?" asked Silver Birch. "He is not in Canterbury Cathedral, not in St. Paul's, not in Westminster. They have driven him out. They have made him inaccessible and beyond the reach of mankind. They have crowned him with Godhood. They have confused the simple minds with doctrines based on fables and myths, and have placed the Nazarene far beyond their reach.

"He is working to serve humanity still. It is all so simple, but they have made it so difficult, so complicated. And they have said that we who teach these truths are the powers of evil masquerading as angels, that this is the voice of Satan, the Prince of Darkness, who teaches you to serve one another and to fight the vested interests of selfishness! But their day is done. They have failed you and have nothing to offer a weary, desolate world."

It seems that the Nazarene presides over the conferences of spirit guides that are held twice a year in the spirit world, at Easter and at Christmas. Silver Birch always suspended his sittings for a few weeks at these times, so he could attend the conferences. He sometimes tried to explain what happens at them. At one sitting, the last before a break, he said:

"This is the greatest pleasure of all, to which I look forward with eager anticipation, when I can become my real self just for a short while and enjoy what is my rightful heritage, to mix with those I have known so well, so long, and to taste life as it is understood only in those spheres where reality is known by those who have a spiritual discernment from years of progress and evolution. I do not speak egotistically. You who live in the world of matter, you who are restricted to five crude senses, you whose spirits are imprisoned in a physical body, you who are limited, you who know not the boundless joys of a freed spirit, you who know only life through its five prison bars, you do not yet realise what life means. You do not know how the spirit, when it find itself, has the freedom to enjoy all the beauties of the Great Spirit that belong to the higher self and the deeper consciousness.

"I go back to my own, to those with whom I have been for many centuries, to taste the life that I knew for so long, that I have willingly abandoned to serve you all. I would not be truthful if I did not say that on this occasion I look forward with joy to all that is in store. As you know, this is our greatest festival of all, when a mighty concourse of all beings, of all races, of all nationalities, all the servers and labourers in the many fields and in many lands, meet to compare their progress. I cannot describe it because there is no language. All the beauties that you have imagined in your greatest moments of inspiration pale into unimportant insignificance beside the reality that is ours on these occasions.

"The greatest joy of all is to make contact once again with the Nazarene—not the Nazarene of the Churches, not the being who has been misrepresented and exalted and deified into an inaccessible and remote position, but the great human spirit who only seeks to inspire service, who wishes to share his greatness with all who desire to serve his Father and our Father."

Silver Birch always took the opportunity, at these last séances before his absence for a few weeks, to speak of the work that had been done through the circle and to give quite unnecessary thanks to the circle members for their loyalty.

"I want you all to know," he said, "that, as the years pass and the bonds of intimate love between us become closer, I pay tribute to the Great Spirit, Who gave me the privilege of serving you and enabled me to win the affection of the loving hearts of those who know me not as I am but who hear me speak to them just once every week and who respect me because they believe and trust me. I am proud of your love and your confidence, and I strive always to say nothing and to do nothing that in any way shall mar the great affection that I know wells up in your hearts towards me.

"I rejoice that our labours have borne so much fruit. I rejoice that so many have found the light of truth because of the little work that we have done. I rejoice because ignorance has been vanquished and superstition compelled to withdraw. I rejoice because truth marches on and we are in the vanguard. I rejoice that you have had stout hearts in the great fight that we have constantly waged and that you have not failed. You have played your part with loyalty and have not betrayed the great trust that has been reposed in you. I rejoice in your service because I see in a humble way the success of my own mission reflected in your labours."

There followed a personal message to each member of the circle, as was Silver Birch's custom on these occasions. When these were finished, he went on:

"Now, with a heart that is a little heavy but with a mind that is joyous in anticipation, I will leave you. I will go and seek refreshment from the fount of all spiritual energy, I will go to seek new inspiration from on high, so that, filled with vitalising power, I may return to be of greater service to you and to manifest, I hope, more of the rich bounty of the infinite Great Spirit. I will take with me all the love of your hearts, all your good wishes, I know, and I will come back to you and I will look forward to meeting you all again. Be full of hope and courage; the snows of winter bring despair, but spring comes in all her fresh garb, arrayed in smiling laughter. Be full of hope and courage; even the darkest night gives way to the glory of the dawn which heralds the rising sun.

"And now, farewell. The Great Spirit bless you and cause the benediction of His infinite love to be showered on you in all its bounty, His spirit radiate through all your spirits and shine triumphantly in the lives that you live. The Great Spirit bless you all. I leave the darkness of your world and greet the light of higher realms. And my last words are the words that I always use when I come. 'The Great Spirit bless you all.'"

After attending one of these spirit-world conferences, Silver Birch commented:

"There I have recaptured some of the glories which once belonged to me. I have been permitted once again to share in the deliberations of those who strive to work for the betterment of your world, to aid progress and whose ambition is to accelerate all the reforms that are so necessary for the well-being of your world. The work that has been done by many of us has been reviewed in all its details and we have been shown how far we have succeeded, and where we have failed. Plans have been made, a programme has been compiled for the work that lies ahead of us, the work that is to be achieved to advance these truths so necessary in the present stage of your world's evolution.

"I have met many whose desire it is to serve you, whom death has not prevented from the labours that lie close to their hearts. And if I may be forgiven a little personal note—a thing of rarity—I am proud to say that I have received some little commendation for the small work I have been able to achieve during the past few months. I feel that I do not deserve it, for I am only the mouthpiece. I have but repeated the message of those who sent me and you have broadcast it.

"These truths which we enunciate have brought knowledge, comfort and cheer to many who knew not where to turn, whose hearts were heavy, filled with grief, in whose eyes there were tears of sorrow."

'To bring the light'

"Let us seek the blessing of the Great Spirit of all. Oh, Great White Spirit, the whole of creation pays homage to Thee, because Thy laws sustain every manifestation of life and all rhythm is but an expression of Thee.

"Thou hast sent into the world of matter at all times instruments who can radiate Thy love, Thy wisdom and Thy knowledge, that they might become living demonstrations of Thy spirit, to being the light of Thy truth into the darkness of men's minds, to illumine all mankind with the rays of Thy infinite wisdom and love.

"Oh, Great Spirit, Thou has sent us as Thy messengers, once again to bring to the children of earth the knowledge of Thee and of Thy laws, that they may understand their relationship with Thee, and so begin to understand themselves and the purpose for which Thou hast placed them in the world of matter.

"We thank Thee because we are able to hold communion

with those susceptible to the things of Thy spirit and whose ears, eyes, minds, hearts and souls are attuned to our larger life and who can listen to the message that Thou wouldst have us proclaim."

Chapter Seven

'THERE IS A PLAN'

THE influence of the spirit world on this earth was touched upon by Silver Birch in replying to a series of questions put by sitters. The guide's medium did not see the questions, which were put to the guide and answered immediately.

"How far do spirit guides influence political systems?" asked one sitter. "Do they mentally suggest lines of advance along the path of brotherhood, or do they impress leaders with specific plans?"

"As you know, we are not concerned with the labels that men wear," said Silver Birch, "or the parties to which they give their allegiance. We are only concerned with service to humanity. We see a world filled with abuse, with iniquity, with vested interests that stand in the way of the unfettered and free distribution of the lavish bounty of the Great Spirit. Therefore we oppose all those who range themselves on the side of selfishness; we wage war on them. We use as our instruments men and women of all parties and of none, of all religions and of none, of all beliefs and of none, wherever we can exert an influence, wherever we can move an individual to labour for reform, for betterment, for amelioration—in one word, for service.

"The Plan is known; what your world should be has been revealed to countless seers and sages, poets, dreamers, idealists, martyrs, all who have sought, because their eyes have seen the vision splendid, to transform a sordid world into a true and real Garden of Eden."

"How much has free will to do with it?" asked a sitter.

"Free will plays a very important part," said Silver Birch. "But remember, when you use the term, you are referring to something that is a contradiction, because no will is entirely free. It is governed by circumstances over which it has no control and to which the will must subordinate itself. Free will is conditioned by the elements, by the laws of your world, by the natural laws of the universe and by the state of your own evolution. We are always trying to throw our influence on the side of everything which is for the progress and the helpfulness of mankind. We cannot interfere with your free will, but we can influence your choice of a better and more rational judgement in life.

"One of the saddest things, as I have told you, is that we are compelled very often to stand helpless, powerless, impotent, watching those we love battling with a problem in life, knowing that at that stage we must not help because on the outcome depends their growth, the unfoldment of their character, the strengthening of their spirit. You have your free will and you decide, in accordance with your mental outlook, your state of evolution, your stage of growth, how to use it. And we are there to help you when we can."

"Do guides work behind the leaders of each country, seeking to inspire them when they are responsive?" was the next question.

"Yes, always," answered the guide, "and it is also true that the natural law of attraction is in operation, because where there is a kinship between the two sets of individuals they automatically desire to help those who are carrying on their work. When there comes to our world a statesman who was in his earth life particularly drawn to some programme of reform, if it is not completed he strives to influence others who show the inclination to continue his reform. And to that extent it is true that for a time nationality operates even in our world, until the spirit outgrows it. It is also true that those who pass through with thoughts of aggrandisement, those who pass as drunkards, those who come to our world as a result of drug-taking, seek to obtain satisfaction through others similarly inclined in your world."

"Is there a spirit plan for each group of countries, suited to their particular needs?" was another point raised.

"There is a plan for all countries, because there is a plan for all life," replied the guide. "All those who have worked in your world do not cease their labours owing to an incident that you call death, a step in eternal life. The love of country does not die and, because it is a genuine love, the power of the individual is still used to give service to that land to which he is attached. With greater evolution, all ideas of nationality, of boundaries, fall apart and there comes a recognition of the common bond of spirit in every child of the Great Spirit. But we use love in all its forms for service. Better that an individual should love at least one land and desire to serve it than that he have no love awakened in his consciousness and give no service at all."

"And what happens if the leaders are not responsive?" asked a sitter.

"Nothing," replied the guide. "But do not forget that there is often an unconscious response, an assimilation of ideas from our world unrecognised by the recipient. Inspiration is not always a conscious process. Usually the instrument only knows that he has received from some source outside of himself a poem, a composition, an idea for a painting, a drama, an essay. The source he does not know; he may not even credit the world of spirit with it. That does not matter as long as the idea bears fruit."

"Do guides work with scientists to inspire developments in research for the benefit of man?" Silver Birch was asked.

"I make bold to claim," responded the guide, "that almost every boon in your world, every invention and discovery has its origin in the realms of spirit. The minds of your world are but the receptacles of the greater minds who use them to confer new benefits to your world of matter. It would not be difficult to show from your records how the great inventions of your world were foretold by spirit intelligences, because they knew of the plans that were originated in our world. But you must remember there is a limit to the amount that can be transmitted. Unfortunately there is so much abuse because of a lack of spiritual growth and understanding. The arts of science are prostituted for destruction instead of being used for reconstruction and as a boon to man."

"Are some of the diabolical inventions of ours inspired from your side?" asked a sitter.

"Yes," said the guide. "Our world is not a world of good people. It is a natural world and, until you stop sending us the bad ones, we can do nothing about it. That is why we strive to abolish the iniquities of your world; that is why we strive to teach the necessity to have character built in your lives so that souls can come here prepared, ready for the tasks that await them, instead of being ill-equipped, undisciplined, unprepared."

'Thou art the law'

Let us seek a blessing from the Great Spirit of all. Oh, Great White Spirit, Thou art the Spirit of all life, for Thy being doth pervade all life and fill all space. Every living thing is a reflection of Thee. Thou art revealed in every manifestation of nature, for all of nature is but a mirror of Thy Spirit.

Oh, Great White Spirit, Thou art the law behind all the universe, whether it be that small portion which has been revealed to human understanding or that greater portion as yet unexpressed in human consciousness.

Thou art in the rays of the sun. Thou art in the morning dew. Thou art in the falling rain. Thou art in the nodding pines. Thou art in the murmuring brooks. Thou art in the splashing rivulets. Thou art in the roar of thunder and the flash of lightning.

Thou art in the song of birds. Thou art in every living, moving thing and Thou art expressed in Thy highest form in the human soul and spirit which seeks to reveal Thy divinity in giving service.

Oh, Great White Spirit, we thank Thee for all the revelations of Thy universe, which Thou hast given to all the peoples of earth in all the ages.

We thank Thee for all the light that has been shed in the dark places, for all the wisdom that has banished ignorance and for all the knowledge that has driven away superstition; for the comfort of Thy spirit to those who are distressed, for the strength which comes from Thee for those who are broken in body and racked with pain.

We thank Thee for the great love that pours from Thy heart and is manifested in Thy servants, who belong to all Thy peoples in Thy many lands. We thank Thee, oh, Great Spirit, for the privilege of serving Thee from the world of spirit, of joining in co-operation with those who are our spiritual kith and kin, so that together we may establish Thy greater kingdom of Spirit in the world of matter.

We thank Thee for all the willing service and the love that flows from human hearts. We thank Thee for all who are linked with us in order to make Thy will manifest on earth.

We pray, oh, Great Spirit, that all the obstacles that prevent the fullest descent of Thy power may be abolished and here in this temple, as in all temples, there shall come the fullest revelation of Thy spirit. This is the prayer of Thy Indian servant, who seeks to serve.

Chapter Eight

'MAN MAY THWART'

DO special days of prayer have any effect? Is there any purpose in Spiritualists, for example, organising one? When these and other pertinent points were put to the spirit sage, he replied:

"Though we laugh, and all is done with such good humour, there is a great and serious purpose behind the task on which we are all engaged. You who come here can never realise the extent to which you have enabled thousands to rejoice because of what you have done. These words, which flow through these lips, part of the message which comes to me to transmit by now have grown customary to you. They form part of the accepted background of your lives. There is nothing new or revolutionary in the things you hear me say.

"Years ago you won your mental and spiritual freedom. You accept as truth that over which your mind has delved and searched for a long time, accepting this, rejecting that, and testing, examining with your reason that the Great Spirit has given you the messages you have heard expressed. You know now that the simple truths we teach are indeed truths which are eternal. But to many others, still wandering in the wilderness of darkness, doubt and difficulty, they come as messengers of liberty, rescuing them from the sorry plight into which they have been plunged for too long. These truths of the spirit are intended to free your world by teaching man how to free himself. Always we begin with the individual, the unit which, when it is multiplied by millions, constitutes the world in which you live. It is a very slow and arduous process, illuminating one by one, but it could not be done otherwise. Mass conversion always fails. When the hypnotic spell is broken and the emotions recede to normal, it is all forgotten. And, indeed, perhaps those who have experienced these heightening calls to their senses are sometimes a little ashamed.

"And so, despite all opposition and hostility and antagonism, we continue to labour, reiterating the simple truths which in the end must prevail, knowing that even as little drops of water will in time wear away a stone, to one by one the light comes and the truth is embraced. Where it is understood and appreciated in all the fulness of its implications, there is to be found a soul who will never look back, who will never regret saying farewell to the bonds that held him for too long. You have moved out of darkness into light. You have seen the light of truth; you have tested it. You know that what we say is reasonable, it does not outrage your common sense, it does not make your intelligence revolt. You are puzzled why all people do not accept what is so crystal clear to you.

"Remember, there are still great hosts arrayed against us—the professional vested interests of the Church particularly, who would do all in their power to resist our mission. They who have nothing to offer your world but antiquated teaching, they who dwell in the past and try to resurrect the splendour of yesterday because they have no glory of today, they whose temples are derelict mausoleums filled with a dreary emptiness where the Great Spirit is not to be found, they are the ones who denounce us and who declare that evil accompanies us, and that we seek to ensnare the gullible and the deluded. We weep over them, the men who often, though they do not know it, betray their calling, who do not lead their flock to the Great Spirit, who build a wall between the Great Spirit and His children, who cling to a book, to a creed, to a church, regarding all these as more important than truth.

"It is to these people that we address words of sternness, seeing in them men who have failed, who are unable to give guidance or a lead in the afflictions that come to thousands. Religion has long since lost its meaning to them. It has been so adulterated with theology that the simple inspiration which their founder gave to the world has been forgotten. The religion we teach is the religion of service, for service is the coin of the spirit. When you serve the children of the Great Spirit, you are serving the Great Spirit and you are indeed religious."

The guide was asked whether, when dealing with the orthodox, it was better to be gentle or harsh.

"Speak the truth, fear no man," he said. "You are a servant of the Great Spirit. Always refute evil, always answer lies. Be fearlesss; there is no need to be afraid. The power that fashioned the universe is not impressed because you build a great cathedral and fill it with beautiful music and have stained glass windows and impressive processions. You cannot imprison the Great Spirit in a building."

Answering another question Silver Birch said: "You can put blinkers on the eyes of the people for a long time and compel them to live in darkness, but one day they remember they are children of the light, and they yearn for the sunshine of truth. You can delay, you can impede, but in the end truth finds its own level everywhere. You are spiritual beings, not bodies of matter alone, and because you are spiritual beings of infinite possibilities, divine in nature, all the powers of the spirit cry out for expression. You can deny them for a while, but you cannot extinguish them. That is why truth must prevail. Because you are spiritual beings the spirit that is within you is part of the power that fashioned the whole mighty universe in all its multitudinous manifestations. No priestcraft can still the voice of the spirit for ever."

Asked whether days of prayer had any effect in the spirit world, Silver Birch replied: "Only insofar as people are of one mind for one little while. But true prayer is something that comes involuntarily from the heart. It is not an organised automatic means of addressing the Great Spirit."

"Would there be any point in Spiritualists holding a day of prayer?" was the next question.

"There is no virtue in those who call themselves Spiritualists unless they are living in their lives the implications of the truth they have received," said the guide. "We do not worship labels. It is not what a man designates himself that matters; it is what he does."

Developing the theme of the failure of Orthodoxy and the growth of spirit truth, Silver Birch said at another meeting of the circle:

"You are beginning to witness some of the processes of crumbling and decay and to see once-proud teachers admitting that they no longer hold any sway over the minds of the people. Those who, for too long, have been blind leaders of the blind, who have foisted their ancient creed and insisted that worship be paid to the God of their creation, who have resisted the upward march of truth and denied the power of the spirit as a living experience of today, are paying the price for their refusal to recognise the efficacy of spiritual law.

"There is a great lesson for you to realise. All those who battle for truth must in the end prevail, for all the forces of goodness cannot be defeated. They may be stayed, they may be impeded, they may be delayed, but none can destroy the truth or prevent her from being established in her rightful place. This is true, not only of religion, but of every aspect of life. Those who desire to resist error, to destroy falsity, to oppose superstition, in every branch of living, must never falter, must pin their complete faith to the great, eternal, infinite power which sustains all life and which assures them of final victory.

"I know how difficult it is for the many who have discovered the truths of spiritual laws which ensure communication between the two states of life to make progress when conditions imposed by war are against them. They must hold fast to that which has been revealed to them. They must hold on to all the knowledge which they have gained, so that when the time is ripe and there is a demand for the floodgates of knowledge to be opened wide, because many will be hungry and thirsty for this truth, they will be able to supply their needs.

"When the conflict ceases, when all the shouts of warfare have died down, there will be many thousands who will want to re-establish their lives on a foundation of knowledge. They will be more than dissatisfied with the ancient fables thrust on them in the name of religion. Having been through the crucible of bitter experience, having faced situations where they have been compelled to question the fundamentals of life, to ask themselves 'Why? How? When?' they will want to know. They will yearn for truth. You must be ready for them, so that hearts which have become bitter, souls which have become dissatisfied, and minds which yearn for knowledge, can come to you and you can, with reason, with confidence, with logic, with truth and wisdom on your side, help them to play their part as citizens of the New World.

"Do not look back too much on the past, except to learn from it the lessons—how failures may be corrected, how mistakes may be avoided. Look towards the future, so that what you do today may prepare you for the greater days that are yet to come. The world will need you. Millions will turn to you for hope and comfort, for inspiration, for guidance. They will not go to churches, they will not go to clergymen, they will not go to priests. They will come to you, for having lived close to death, having experienced some of the laws which operate when death hovers near your world, their eyes will have become opened. The mist which has caused partial blindness will have fallen away. They will be ready, and you must be ready, too."

When asked, "How do you see a new world being born?" the guide replied:

"I see a plan, a divine plan. I see that power of the spirit is the greatest power of the universe. Man may thwart and delay, man may impede and stay, but man cannot forever prevent the power of the spirit being made manifest. When you have the knowledge of spiritual truth, you have the key which unlocks all the doors of mankind's problems. I am not being unkind to all the sincere reformers who, moved by anger, by righteous wrath, or by an overwhelming sympathy for the downtrodden and the weak, seek to repress wrong, to fight injustices, to enable all the bounties of the Great Spirit to be fairly distributed. They see only one part of a problem. They see physical needs that must be satisfied—perhaps they see mental needs that must be satisfied, too—but pre-eminently man is a spirit, part of the Great Spirit, part of the power which fashioned all life. Man is not so infinitesimal that he is forgotten amidst the vast spaces of the universe. He is always part of the Great Spirit, contributing to the spiritual nature of Infinity.

"You cannot stifle the power of the spirit; it must emerge. It will triumph over cruelty and hatred, it will triumph over bludgeons, concentration camps, dictators, because the spirit of man must be as free as the air which he breathes. That is his natural, divine, spiritual heritage. All those who have seen the vision splendid, and have beheld the new world that is to be, know that it must be, because it is part of that same purpose which breathed into man and raised him from animal to human—and will raise him again from human to divine. Your task is always to hand on the torch, rekindle its flame, so that the generation which comes after you will have a greater light to illuminate its pathway. The foundations have been laid. They were laid many years ago in our world. And gradually, painfully, laboriously, men and women of all denominations, and of none, were raised up to be witnesses to the eternal spirit, to labour for the quickening of the divine plan. The new world must come."

"If the new world has got to come by the result of our own efforts," asked one member of the circle, "why should the new world be born in your world?"

"Your world is the shadow; the light is cast in ours," was the spirit answer. "You are executing plans which you have helped to create and bring to fruition in your own world. All the original work, if you like to use those words, is done in our world, because all the energising, all the dynamic, originates, not with matter, but with spirit. You are all instruments, whether you are conscious of this fact or not. You receive and transmit. And according to the degree that you make yourselves susceptible to spirit influence, so are you successful or not."

"So the new world is to be born through our own endeavours allied to yours," commented this sitter.

"Yes," said the guide, "because no one works alone. Wherever an effort is put forth it is always by our effort. We have to find instruments. You have to attune yourselves to the power which can flow through you. Perfection is never achieved. There is an eternal process at work smoothing away all the difficulties, getting rid of all the obstacles."

"We ourselves should earn our own earthly new world," declared another member of the circle.

"It can only come when you have earned it," agreed Silver Birch. "I can only say to you, here are things which must be achieved because they are part of the plan. But your co-operation will determine the time it takes. There is a plan, but it is not automatic. It is subject to your free will. You are co-operators, you are not automatons, puppets or marionettes. You are part of the Great Spirit."

"You have been saying that a new world is coming," asserted another, "but we ourselves see hardly any sign of it at all."

But the guide answered: "As fast as the old order crashes so does the new begin. Have you not seen the processes of disintegration before your eyes? Great empires have fallen. The power of money is no longer supreme. It has been proved that selfishness does not pay. The common man and woman have demonstrated the sterling qualities that can be called forth in service. Do not tell me that no progress has been made. The lesson is before your eyes. You require no power of clairvoyance to see it. It is there. The people deserve the new world. If they are denied it, it is because they are not exercising the power which is theirs. They have earned it by their sacrifice.

"I do not say that it will be a mechanical process, but potentially all is ready. You must play your part, and it is done by spreading knowledge, by waging war on all those vested interests that will cling with greedy fingers to every vestige of an old order."

Hundreds of questions have been submitted to Silver Birch. He liked them, but excepting his private messages, he answered only impersonal ones, for he stated that to deal with personal problems he would require to have before him the one who was perplexed, and that was not his real work, which is teaching. One of the questions put to him was, "Is it possible for you to give some new truth?" This was his reply:

"There is no new truth. Truth is truth. There is knowledge which depends upon the individual being ready to receive it. When you are children you are taught according to your capacity to assimilate. You begin with the letters of your alphabet and, as the mind grows, you are taught to make words and to read. Gradually the knowledge contained in the printed word becomes accessible to you. As to the amount of knowledge that you receive, that is dependent wholly and solely upon your capacity for appreciating it. There is an infinity of wisdom, range upon range upon range, but it can only become available to you as you are mentally and spiritually equipped to receive it.

"But no knowledge alters truth. There is no wisdom that in any way alters the truth of any teaching. If it was true in the past it is true today and will be true tomorrow. Truth is constant and eternal. You can add to wisdom, you can add to knowledge, but you cannot bring new truth. Your world has all the truth that it requires for its essential purpose—the fundamental truths of kindness, service, love. It knows what it should do in order to have a better world. All that is necessary for your growth, progress, unfoldment, evolution has been made known throughout all the generations. If man would but follow the truth which has been revealed he could achieve here and now on earth far more of the divinity within him than has ever been manifested.

"All the great teachers, the instruments of the spirit who have added their lustre to the world, have taught truths that were similar in basis. Each came to reveal the spiritual nature of man, to draw attention to the eternal qualities possessed by every human being. Each taught of the infinite soul, the divine spark, the portion of the Great Spirit resident within all human life. Each taught those principles which, if adopted and followed, would enable that spirit to have a greater expression. Each made it clear that living according to spiritual ideals would banish from your world all the miserable spectres that haunt it, all the fears and miseries and sadnesses which have needlessly afflicted it for too long.

"Love thy neighbour as thyself, give service to those who need it, help the weary and the thirsty, heal the sick, comfort the mourner, visit those who are in affliction—these are the truths that have been taught a long time ago. If man would but practise them he could transform the whole of his world and make it impossible for war, with all its hideous horrors, to be visited on him again. Let me make it clear what is our attitude. It is that man has at his command all that which is necessary for his growth and for his spiritual equipment. There are many sacred books, there have been many teachers, many inspired men and women who have caught glimpses of the inner life and each in his own way has interpreted what he has seen. But, unfortunately, the simple truth which has been revealed from the higher aspects of life has been overlaid. Men have built on it edifices of doctrine, of dogma, of creed, of ritual, of ceremony. A whole bulwark of theology has been placed on the foundation of simple spiritual truth until now the foundations are completely forgotten. Thus it is that we have constantly sought out instruments through whom the message of the spirit could be given in all its pristine beauty, in all the quality of its simplicity, radiant because it is unadorned.

"We are not concerned with systems of belief fashioned by the minds of man, we are concerned with the truths of the spirit as they have been revealed in the world of spirit where we are not confronted with the illusions of your earthly life. It is because we have seen so many human wreckages, so many human derelicts coming to our world, it is because we have seen the transition of so many thousands completely unfitted in every way for the life that confronts them, ignorant, full of misconception, filled with prejudice, that we decided that it would be far simpler if man, whilst on earth, could have in his midst the simple truth that would prepare him for that life which one day will be his abiding reality. And so we have declared constant war on all those systems and organisations, on all those beliefs which stand in the way, all the obstacles that have needlessly been created, all the superstitions which becloud and befuddle the mind, so that all the children of the Great Spirit can have at their command the eternal truths which will enable them to live their lives as the Great Spirit intended that they should.

"Never mind what others say, forget all the condemnations and all the denunciations. These are the simple truths of the spirit that will stand forever. They will answer every test that reason demands. They will not demean your intelligence. They are simple, so simple, that they can be grasped and understood by any ordinary individual. These are the truths that will prevail long after all priestcraft has completely failed—simple, eternal truths of the spirit, founded on the eternal, natural laws. We require no popes, no archbishops, no priests, no clergymen, no churches, no temples, no synagogues. We build no system of theology. We enunciate simple truths and we are determined that, given the instruments, these simple truths will continue to permeate every form of society, so that all men can be free in body, mind and spirit, and never again shall they become bondmen living in slavery. The darkness of ignorance will have perished and the light, the effulgent light of truth, will reign in its place."

Another time, speaking of the aid which comes from the spirit world to those then at war and fighting for human liberty, Silver Birch said:

"We have to wage war on needless ignorance. It is not part of the plan of the Great Spirit that His children, filled with the essence of His divinity, who exist because part of the divine spirit is immanent within them, should live their lives in the obscurity of ignorance, walking always in the shadows and the mists, seeing no purpose and no direction, asking questions to which they think there can be no answers. There is an infinite storehouse of knowledge which is placed at the disposal of all who desire to have it, but it must be earned by growth and struggle, by evolution and progress.

"The soul must fit itself, the mind must ripen, the heart must be ready and prepared so that the knowledge can find a dwelling-place within. You can receive only that which you can bear to receive. The blind man who is about to see can only have the vision given to him in small degrees, for if suddenly he were able to view the whole of that which is round and about him, grave damage would be done. So it is with the truths of the spirit. Gradually as you mount the rungs of the ladder, you draw nearer and nearer and you accumulate some grains of wisdom.

"Once you display any initiative, and reveal by your actions and by your thoughts that you are ready and receptive, then you begin to harmonise and attune yourself with the processes which enable you to receive that knowledge and teaching for the stage you have reached. There are no final boundaries, there are no limits beyond which man cannot go, for he is infinite, and knowledge is infinite, too. But it is not only ignorance that we have to fight.

"We have to wage war on all those forces and organisations which have for centuries deliberately encouraged the children of the Great Spirit to dwell in the darkness, who have by every means in their power, compelled those over whom they held dominion to accept that which they propounded as truth and tried to prevent truth from spreading. We look back through the ages and see how, despite every attempt made from our world to aid man in his struggle for liberty and enfranchisement, we have had to combat the forces of so-called religion which, instead of aiding the soul in its natural desire for freedom have resisted any attempt at the gates of the prison being opened.

"There are still remnants of the opposition today. There are still those, either knowingly or unconsciously, who range themselves against the forces of light, who denounce us with harshness, bitterness and rancour, who oppose every effort to destroy the false creeds in which many of them no longer themselves believe, who cling to their sacerdotalism, who will not relinquish that which they regard as their privilege and who pay allegiance to threadbare theological shibboleths. We come to reveal that there is a large and wondrous life of the spirit which beats restlessly and surges, so that the barriers can be broken down, so that the vast power of the spirit, that energising, dynamic, vital, life-giving force, can be placed at the disposal of all. It has inspired many in days gone by; it can inspire and will inspire many again.

"There is much work to be done in a world filled with devastation; there is so much sorrow and sadness, weeping and tribulation, so many who feel their lives are aimless, so many who are bowed down with grief and do not know where to turn. To all of these, the power of the spirit, invisible though it may be, can prove that it is the abiding reality which will comfort them, inspire them, cherish them and lead them so that all who need the guidance shall receive it.

"That is the part which can be played by all who have received the knowledge and who dedicate their lives to be instruments of the new, yet old, dispensation, so that they can spread the gospel of liberation, the evangel of freedom, and cause all those who are weary and downcast to lift up their hearts and to know the greater glory that could be theirs. It is the power of the spirit that we offer, the power of the spirit which can triumph over every difficulty, conquer every obstacle and reveal the light of truth, wisdom and understanding and enable the children of the Great Spirit to build systems of enduring peace."

Answering a comment made by one member of the circle, Silver Birch said: "Learn the secret of obtaining refreshment for the mind and spirit. You must not be so busy that you neglect the fundamentals of your own being. You have within yourself the means of recuperation, the power that will bring you vitality when you are tired.

"Withdraw for a few moments into the quietness and solitude of your own being so that you can allow the spirit to be at one with the elemental forces of life which are round and about you. When you are passive and attuned to them, they will bring you all the vigour, they will recharge you and enable you to face a new day with more strength than you had before."

"Do spirit people always know in advance the time when people on earth will pass over even if they are killed in war?" was the next inquiry.

"Some people in my world know, but how far in advance they know depends upon a variety of circumstances," replied the guide. "They always know when they are associated by ties of love when the final dissolution will take place, because it becomes part of their willing task to aid the spirit to free itself from its physical body. But the fact is not known to everybody who is now in the world of spirit. No one who dies, to use your language, ever dies alone. Always, without any exception, there is a company of their own beloved to help them across the border, to receive the soul which has passed through the valley of shadows to begin the new and wondrous epoch of its life."

Silver Birch always insisted that he is the teacher of simple spirit truths. He once refused to answer an involved question, "not because I wish to shirk the issue, but I am restricting myself to the dispensing of that information which is of immediate application. When you see so many ignorant of the veriest simplicities, who do not know the elementary beginnings, I do not think it wise to deal with the deeper issues that can bide their time.

"The paramount need of today is for the dissemination of those simple truths, assurance of the life beyond the grave, assurance that you are never friendless, neglected or lonely, assurance that there is an overruling, guiding, beneficent power filled with the warmth of divine love. These are the things which all should know. These are the priceless possessions which are available to all. And when there are thousands, tens of thousands, maybe hundreds of thousands, who are ignorant of these elementary truths, let us think of them first, for they are our primary duty."

Developing this theme at another séance, the guide said:

"The whole purpose of our return has been misconstrued by those who should be the leaders in all matters of religion. Primarily throughout all the ages, religion has been associated with the power of the spirit. It had its beginning in the fact that always there returned from my world teachers appointed to instruct the children of earth in all the laws that control and regulate their spiritual growth. The whole purpose of religion concerns itself with the spirit of man. That is its beginning, and religion is intended to convey what man should do in order that his spirit shall receive the exercise that will enable it to achieve its rightful growth. There is a whole range of spiritual law, but unfortunately it has been misinterpreted and there has been confusion entirely due to the intervention of priestcraft which had its own ends to serve.

"Primarily man is a spirit with a body, not a body with a spirit. The body is subservient to the superior spirit. The whole purpose of earthly life is to provide the training for the indwelling spirit, so that through a variety of experiences it can be matured, it can fit itself, it can prepare for the day, the day of liberation brought by death, when it starts its real career. Religion, therefore, is that set of precepts, that code of ethics, which enables the spirit to live as it should live.

"Now unfortunately, in days gone by, there was a clash between the instrument of the spirit (the medium) and the priest, whose task originally was to concern himself with the function of the temples or the churches, the buildings where religious practices were carried out. The two first worked side by side, and then the priest resented the attention paid to the one through whom inspiration came. There began that long process of theology, of the classification and creed, of ritual, of ceremony, of dogma, of doctrine, none of which has any real connection today with the gifts of the spirit or its life or its development.

"And so real religion has become obscured today. Those who think of religion think of it in terms of certain set ceremonies; they think of readings from books regarded as sacred, they chant certain hymns, they wear certain vestments. They give

their allegiance to certain forms of words and cling to them
long after reason has dictated they are fallacious. We are not
concerned with any theology, we are not concerned with any
creed, with any formula of any kind.

"We are concerned primarily with the spirit of man, and the
whole of our teaching is directed to those natural laws to which
we give our allegiance. That which man has made we cannot
worship. That which the Great Spirit has created we know to
be true. Therein is the chief difference in our approach to
religion. We say that service, the exercise of the spirit, deeds
which are unselfish and altruistic, the attempt to help those less
fortunate than yourself, giving strength to the weak, removing
the load off the shoulders of those who have much to carry—all
this to us is religion.

"It is not religion or religious to declare that the Great Spirit
is 'Three in One or One in Three.' That does not increase the
growth of the spirit by one iota. You may sing hymns from
sunrise to sunset, but that will not make you any more spiritual.
You may read the Bible, or the Talmud, or the Koran, or the
Bhagavad-Gita, or any sacred book until your eyes grow
weary, but that will not increase the growth of your spirit. You
may do all things that men regard as religious, but unless they
inspire you to lead better lives, unless they enable the spirit
within you to find greater expression, then you are not religious
as we see it.

"We are concerned with deeds, with actions and with the life
that every individual lives. We teach the supreme law of cause
and effect, that none thwarts the Great Spirit, that none cheats
the law, that man is his own saviour and his own redeemer, that
man pays the penalty for every wrongdoing, and that man reaps
the reward for every kindness that he performs. We say that the
laws of the Great Spirit are mechanical, automatic in their
action; that kindness, tolerance, sympathy, service, automatically
make you the better because you have practised them, and that

selfishness, wrong-doing and intolerance automatically make you worse. You cannot alter that inflexible law. There is no cheap reprieve, there are no easy pardons. Divine justice rules the whole universe. A spiritual dwarf cannot pretend to be a spiritual giant. There is no death-bed repentance."

This is how Silver Birch give his interpretation of the laws that regulate all life, contrasting them with the orthodox view taught for centuries all over the world:

"Let us consider the unchanging, inflexible, omnipotent laws of the Great Spirit which are responsible for all that transpires throughout the whole wide universe. We constantly refer to those laws, for we do not teach of a God who is a person, subject to human weaknesses, human passion, human anger, one who has favourites, who loves some and despises others. We see the universe ruled by laws, laws that have always controlled every facet, laws that will always be in existence.

"It is by teaching your world that all which it sees, all which it knows, is due to these laws, that it will abolish the misconceptions and the falsities, the prejudices and the ignorance which for too long have held man in subjection and slavery. As a knowledge of these laws increases so man's life will become richer in understanding. The veil which prevents him from seeing the full beauty of living will be removed and he will catch glimpses of that greater life which lies beyond the ken of his mortal existence.

"And so we always render our homage and our tribute to the eternal, natural laws of the Great Spirit, the laws which never fail, the laws which never err, the laws which take care of every being, no matter how exalted or inferior his state may be. None is neglected, none is overlooked, none is forgotten, none is lonely. There are no people who are outside or beyond the scope of these laws. The mere fact of their existence is due to the operation of natural laws. Man's laws may fail, man's laws may change, man's laws may be repealed or superseded as growth and development enlarge his vision, as knowledge dispels ignorance, as changing circumstances demand the provision of new ordinances, but there are no additions to the laws of the Great Spirit, there are no revisions, there are no alterations. All the laws that are in operation today, have always been in operation and always will be in operation. They are constant and immutable."

'Thou art in all life'

"Oh, Great White Spirit, Thou Art the source of all things. Thou art the beginning. Thou art the end. Thou art in all, manifested in every phase, whether it is in the highest realms of spirit or the lowest planes of matter. Thou art in the light as Thou are in darkness.

"Thou art in Spring as Thou art in Autumn. Thou art in Summer as Thou art in Winter. Thou art in sunshine as Thou art in storm. Thou art in the flash of lightning, in the roar of thunder. Thou art in the rustle of the winds.

"Thou art in the song of birds. Thou art in the trembling of leaves. Thou art in the murmuring of brooks. Thou art in the heights of mountains. Thou art in the depths of oceans. Thou art in the myriads of suns. Thou art in all the stars.

"Thou art in all life, whether it be life manifested in the highest or expressed in the lowest. Thou art in all consciousness.

"Thou art in all love and hate. Thou art in all wisdom and foolishness. Thou art within and without, for Thou art the Great Spirit of all, without Whose laws nothing can exist.

"Oh, Great White Spirit. Thou art so great that Thou canst not be expressed in the language of earth. Thou canst not be realised to the full even by the highest of the high and the greatest of the great.

"Thou hast been worshipped in all ages and all languages.

Thou hast been revealed by all people and in many books. Thou hast shown Thy laws to all, at every age, who have been enabled to pierce the fog of matter and see with the eyes of spirit.

"Once again, oh, Great Spirit, Thou hast revealed Thyself through Thy spirit messengers to the children of earth, seeking to use them to bring them nearer to Thee, so that they may understand Thee and use Thy power to bring peace and plenty and happiness into the world of matter.

"We who seek to serve Thee would co-operate with the children of earth to spread Thy light into the darkness and make Thy power, Thy love and Thy laws known throughout the whole length and breadth of Thy universe. This is the prayer of Thy Indian servant, who seeks to serve Thee by serving Thy children."

Chapter Nine

'SPIRIT IS LIFE'

THOUGH spirit teaching is simple, not all are content it should so remain! One questioner seemed to have set a poser when he asked Silver Birch, "What is the object of creation?" To this he added, "As Spiritualists teach that man can be gradually improved and absorbed into the Godhead, why create man?" To that the guide replied:

"I am not one of those who teach that mankind is finally absorbed into the Great Spirit. I have always said that I know nothing of finality. I know nothing of a beginning, I know nothing of an end. To me there always has been and there always will be. I see the whole of life on your planet, as well as on other planets, and throughout the realm of spirit, as a constant stream of evolution, with the consciousness slowly rising towards its summit. I know nothing of a birth and consciousness.

"I know nothing of consciousness achieving perfection. I do not think that perfection or absorption is ever accomplished, for as the soul rises higher in the scale of values, as it casts out the dross of past imperfections, so it realises the need for greater progress. The more you evolve the more you see there is to be evolved. The higher you rise, the further away do you see the other heights which are yet to be scaled.

"I am concerned with the development and unfoldment of the consciousness which is part of the Great Spirit in life. This consciousness, as far as I know, always existed, but as it manifests through many varied and diverse forms, constantly improving through its expressions, so it exhibits more and more of its hidden and latent divinity.

"That consciousness has been manifested through all the phases of life, and is still being manifested. That which is now displayed through man has been exhibited through animal, through bird, through fish, through vegetable, through all that is regarded as inanimate life. The consciousness continues to evolve and grow, unfold and expand, becoming more divine and less earthly as it continues its path of evolution. That is the whole purpose of creation, a continual expression in many and varied manifestations of the consciousness which is the Great Spirit. To that I would add always the thought that man must not separate himself or think in terms of separation from the work of creation, because he is part of creation. The creative forces operate through him. His life, his effort, his struggle, contribute to infinite creation.

"Every life can add its quota. And the higher the life, the more altruistic, the more unselfish, the more does it add beauty to the varied manifestations of creation. Not only does the artist, the musician and the poet add his contribution of lustre, but every life can bring an inflection of beauty if it chooses."

From discussion on creation to a question on vibration is a normal transition, and when the query was posed, "Will you give a simple explanation of the term used so much in Spiritualism, 'vibrations'?" this was the answer:

"Wherever you have life you have movement, you have rhythm, you have pulsation, you have vibration. Life cannot be motionless, static or inert. Life is associated always with movement. To understand movement, to measure movement, you have to define it. We speak of vibration, referring to life as being revealed in waves of energy, that bring one of the modes or manifestations of life. Everything which exists vibrates, radiates and is active. Our impingement on your world is due to vibration. We normally vibrate in a world beyond the boundaries of your physical senses. It is a higher octave, if you like, a higher vibration. All the forces, all the power, all the manifestations of the spirit are accomplished by more delicate, subtle vibrations.

"To make your world, engrossed and encased in matter as it is, repond, one of two things has to happen. Either you must raise your slower vibrations, or we must lower our quicker vibrations. It is fairly easy to see that we could meet half-way. Alas, alas, it is usually we who have to come all the way, for very little contribution is made by your world. To speak through this instrument I have to slow down my vibrations. When I return to the spheres, discarding the personality through which I manifest, I have to accelerate my vibration to manifest some of the consciousness which belongs to a higher state of being and activity. It is caused by vibration. It is the only word which succinctly explains our activity. It is interesting to note that so many scientists, who for years have turned deaf ears and blind eyes to the whole realm of spiritual activity, now, in their examination of a world of matter, are beginning to realise that its secrets are to be discovered in vibrations."

When the subject of prayer was raised again, the guide answered:

"To appreciate prayer, you must realise its purpose. The mere mouthing of words, the mere repetition of a formula achieves nothing. These well-worn tracks in the atmosphere attract nobody, neither do they create any vibrant forces. We are not intereted in stereotyped phrases, for there is no sincerity behind them and the one who utters them usually does so with indifference, for he has long ceased to ponder on the meaning of the words that are repeated almost as an automaton. There is, however, some value in real prayer. It is never suggested that whilst you live in your world any action of the mind can be a substitute for the labours that you have to perform.

"Prayer is not intended to be a refuge of the coward who seeks to escape his obligations. Prayer is not a substitute for the work that you have to do. Prayer is not a means by which you can escape your responsibilities. Prayer is not a means of outwitting the laws of the Great Spirit. No prayer can do that, neither can it by one iota make any alteration in the unbreakable sequence of cause and effect.

"You can disregard all prayers that do not spring from a heart which is willing to serve and which is conscious of its obligations and its duties. Having disregarded all those, there are the prayers which, because they are a psychic or spiritual exercise, set into motion certain vibrations which bring responses. Those responses are not necessarily the ones for which the man who makes the prayer expects, but they are the natural result of the vibrations he has created.

"If you have faced honestly, fairly and squarely all the problems and difficulties that beset you; if you have tried within the limits of your own power to find a solution and you have failed, then you have a perfect right to ask that some higher power, some greater soul, should give you light in your hour of perplexity. And you will get that guidance, you will get that light, for those who are round and about you, those who see with the eyes of the spirit, know the conditions of your own soul. They know, for example, whether you are honest or not.

"Then there is the prayer of those who desire to effect a more complete harmony with the spiritual forces of life, the prayer of the soul which yearns to overcome the barriers imposed by the physical body and seeks to claim its own. Those prayers must be answered, for their mere exercise is enabling the spirit gradually to acquire its rightful heritage. Always when you speak of prayer, you must differentiate between the kinds of prayer to which you are referring.

"Now I come to what is called the Lord's Prayer, and I immediately say that no stereotyped prayer has any value for mankind, that the mere act of formality robs it of any potency that originally it may have possessed. It may serve as a useful formula, but it cannot help you in any other way. The Great

Spirit is perfect law. It is not necessary to besiege the Great Spirit with requests which you can answer. Then you must remember, too, that many years have rolled by since the days when the Nazarene is supposed to have uttered it. Man has grown and evolved and realises far more about life in many of its ramifications. Not quite in that form was it expressed by the Nazarene, but it was clothed in the language which was applicable to the people of his day.

"Now you know that the Great Spirit is not in heaven—being the perfect law the Great Spirit pervades all space, all life; there is no aspect of life in the mighty universe of which the perfect law is not cognisant. The Great Spirit is no more in the highest heaven than the Great Spirit is in the lowest hell. The Great Spirit is universal and is manifested through every phase of universal activity. There is no necessity to address petitions announcing that the kingdom of the Great Spirit will come; that will happen, but as to when it will happen depends upon the labour of those who are co-operating with the power of the spirit and who seek to advance its coming. That it will come is inevitable, but whether that coming is hastened or delayed depends upon the work that people in your world are able to do."

When Silver Birch was asked what he thought of the Ten Commandments, he agreed that they were out of date; it was suggested he should draw up another set of commandments.

"You must not regard the power of the spirit as it was expressed in any period of man's long history as being the final word in all divine revelation," said the guide. "Your world must realise that revelation is continuous and progressive, fitting itself to the stage of understanding of the people to whom it comes. It must not be so far ahead of them that they cannot understand it. It must only be so much in front that it is within their grasp. Always the wisdom of the power of the spirit is but one step ahead, and when man achieves that step, he is ready for the next in the infinite ladder of wisdom. Why should that which obtained in the days when the race was still in its comparative infancy, and had special application to people governed by special conditions, be made to fit circumstances of today which are vastly different? But I have only one commandment, that you serve one another, that is all."

"What is the power of the spirit; is it tangible; can it be described?" When this composite question was put to Silver Birch he replied:

"You use words that are difficult to interpret. When you say 'tangible' what do you mean? Do you mean does it conform to any perception by the five senses? No, it does not. Is it real? Yes, it is as real as knowledge, as real as wisdom, as real as evolution, as real as friendship, as real as love, as real as any invisible force that exists. It is tangible to our plane of expression, but imperceptible except to those who are sensitive and can appreciate its reality. It is a power, a divine power, a power which operates in many lives. Those who are ignorant, those who are prejudiced, those who allow their lives to be ordered by superstition, provide mental barriers, each of which is an obstacle to the power of the spirit, and the nature of the obstacle determines the time that it will take to break it down.

"There are some people who go through the whole of earthly life without having any inkling of the truth. They are unaware that life is spirit, that spirit is life, that the whole of your world depends for its maintenance upon the power of the spirit. These people are deaf, blind and dumb to the realities of spirit, and they live in this material prison until death releases them. And even then, as you know, there is a long process of adjustment before they are able to appreciate reality. Others receive occasional glimpses and in these fleeting moments are aware of that higher, transcendental power which shapes and governs and guides all the processes of life.

"And then there are those who, like yourselves, have received direct knowledge and are accessible to the power of the spirit day by day. You have opened your hearts, your minds, your souls and you are ready to become instruments of that same power which sustains the whole of life and which now seeks to be used through you so that others can be touched and quickened by it. It is all part of one power. The power that regulates all the processes of life is part of that power which we use and is used here to enable me to speak."

In answer to another question Silver Birch said to the members of the home circle: "Have faith, not blind faith, but faith founded on knowledge. Have confidence. It is the old, old cry. It is nothing new I have to tell you, but I do reiterate it with all the eloquence at my command so that it shall become part of the very fabric of your being. Have confidence. You do your part, we will do ours. We shall not fail you. There is a vast range of inspiration that you can have access to if you so desire, but fear, doubt, uncertainty, these are discords that interfere and should have no place in your consciousness. There is a lot of work to be done. I want you to help me by your faithful constancy of purpose. There are many obstacles that even I, with all my long experience, find difficult to conquer. You must help me by being faithful and confident and above all, fearless, by not allowing any thoughts of fear, no worry or anxiety to take root in your being.

"Problems will cross your path, but you will cross them; they will not stay. There will be no difficulty so great that you cannot solve it, no load so heavy that you cannot bear it upon your shoulders. Have no fear. Face whatever the morrow brings you with a resolute heart and a determined spirit and all will be well. There are many thousands who will seek your aid and you must be ready to help them and thus fulfil the purpose of your own existence, for when all is said and done unless you serve, unless you give to others that which you have received, you are not living in your lives the implications of the knowledge that has been vouchsafed to you. There is much to be done. Let us with joyful anticipation take up our task knowing that here and there will be souls who will rejoice because of what we have done."

Two members of the circle were discussing the value of propaganda as they waited for the guide to manifest through the medium and when he had done so, Silver Birch said:

"Why do you think that we have returned—to impart our knowledge to a few or to the many? Is ours a truth to be reserved for those who will keep it to themselves in small councils, in secret societies, reserved just for a handful? Do we not see teeming millions, ignorant, despairing, heart-broken? Ours is a great message, for we strive to reveal all the noble qualities of the Great Spirit that are enshrined within every being in the world. We have to teach them the laws of life—life physical, life mental and life spiritual. We have to make them realise the purpose of their being, the reason for their existence on earth, their latent powers, their divine potentialities, the service they can render, the world they can fashion, the knowledge they can accumulate, the heights they can attain.

"Our truth is destined to reach, in the end, every living soul and to reach them whilst they are still on earth, so that they may learn the lessons and begin to apply the truths of the spirit to the world in which they live. Years and centuries are wasted in repairing wrongs, in making good deficiencies, in retribution, in atonement for all that has been foolishly done. All this time could be saved, all this effort could be directed into other channels if your world were not so pitifully steeped in ignorance.

"You have this knowledge. You know now a little more about the laws of the spirit. You have enjoyed the beauties of spirit communion. You have been united once again with the ones you love, who some of you thought were lost and gone for

ever. You have seen part of the vast divine plan. You have
marvelled at its beauty, at its conception. You have witnessed
some of the workings caused by the power of the spirit. You
have had the joys of inspiration from larger souls. You have
had a higher access to the fountain of knowledge—and for
what? So that you should enjoy these pleasures for yourself?

"But no; knowledge brings responsibility. You in turn must
spread it wherever you can. Whatsoever joy you have received,
it is your duty to pass it on to others so that they too may
become accessible to the power of the spirit, so that others may
learn of the love that awaits them from higher realms, so that
others can be touched by this mighty power that raises men and
women up to become instruments of the mighty purpose of the
Great Spirit of all life.

"Renounce all those who attempt to restrict knowledge.
Knowledge must spread freely so that it will destroy ignorance,
superstition, and all that which for too long has held men in the
chains of bondage. Knowledge will bring them freedom so that
the soul can enjoy the liberty which is its rightful divine
heritage. How foolish are they who see only the light of the
candle when they could behold the radiance of the sun! You are
all instruments, as I am but an instrument, and our task is to
liberate minds everywhere. Thus shall your world make
progress, and men and women fashion systems of life that will
endure and enable all the children of the Great Spirit to enjoy
their existence according to the plan which is founded on
spiritual law."

This is how Silver Birch expressed himself on his outlook and
his mission:

"I am only interested in the truth. The truth is all-important.
I am concerned only with service and helping your world to
understand those spiritual, eternal principles on which a new
world is being built. All those who deviate from this great task

are frittering away energies which should be devoted to the service of their fellow-men and fellow-women. The whole purpose of our return is to act as an incentive to all who will listen, so that they can play their part in the regeneration of your world.

"Too much blind obedience is given to formulas. Too much attention is paid to conventions. I am not concerned with anything but the spread of knowledge and the use of knowledge for the enlightenment of those who are still in darkness. I know only of one religion; it is service. We judge by action, by life, by motive. If those who have this knowledge are to succeed in the task, which is part of the plan, then they must beware of imposing their own boundaries and attempting to restrict the flow of the power of the spirit into channels into which they think it should flow. The power of the spirit cannot be restricted or commanded. It flows wherever there are instruments through whom it can be expressed. We want instruments, mediums, men and women who will allow that power to touch them, who are so constituted that the voice of the spirit can be heard through them, and knowledge that is waiting to be transmitted can be poured through them. These are the urgent tasks.

"Why do we come back for you? Our work is concerned with the millions who, if they had this knowledge in your world, would not come to us derelicts, wrecks, almost unfitted for the life of the spirit. They are filled with ignorance and fear, superstition and prejudice. Our task is to break down all the forces which make for darkness in human life. I never call it Spiritualism. I speak of the natural law. I never say Father God. I speak of the Great Spirit. I see a law: I see a purpose. You have to grow in spiritual stature, and if you would accomplish at least part of that task in your earthly life, then you would be prepared and equipped for the fuller life which is your inevitable destiny. That is why we come back to you; because we love you; because the ties of affectionate kinship bind us together, so that we can serve you and help you to be ready to serve others when your turn comes.

"I can only tell you the truth, as I see it, and always make my appeal to reason, which I have enthroned as the supreme arbiter. Spread knowledge, destroy superstition, help the light to grow and the darkness to recede. Destroy vested interest. Help to kill greed, avarice, self-interest, orthodoxy, convention. These are all the enemies of the spirit. They must go. These are all the hindrances to the new world. All who stand in the way are by their very actions thwarting, for a time, the plan of the Great Spirit of all life. Truth is more important than any organisation.

"The issues are always so simple, but the people of your world do not like simplicity. They like form and convention; they like to copy and to imitate. Because others have built churches, they too must have churches. Because other services begin with a prayer, they too must have a prayer. Because others sing hymns, they too must have hymns, and often the same hymns with alterations. Because others have a sermon, they too must have a sermon.

"But meeting-places exist, when they are dedicated to the power of the spirit, for the spread of knowledge of the Great Spirit and the laws of the spirit. That is all that matters. The bricks do not matter. Buildings do not matter. Do not worship them. Your allegiance should be to the Great Spirit of life and to His eternal, natural laws. The task of all those who have this knowledge is to keep the flame of spirit truth alight, so that there are those who provide hope and comfort and inspiration for the many who know not where to turn. Your world is full of darkness. There are so many who are weary, tired and perplexed, who yearn for one grain of comfort, for one particle of knowledge. These are the ones who require your urgent attention. These are the ones amongst whom you should be busy, telling them of truths that will be like a rock on which they can build the whole of their lives."

'Drive away all weakness'

"Oh, Great White Spirit, Thou art the law, the wisdom, the love, the knowledge and the inspiration.

"We praise Thee because Thou art the centre of all life, for with Thee there is life and without Thee there is nought for Thou dost pervade all life and thy laws sustain and embrace all. We know that thou hast placed within all human life a portion of Thy spirit, which brings all peoples together in unity with Thee.

"And so, Great Spirit, we do not pray to Thee on bended knee, cringing with fear, ashamed of our inheritance, but we pray to Thee with knowledge and in the light of all that we have received, knowing that we are part of Thee and Thou art part of us. We stand before Thee, children of Thee, knowing that Thy spirit is within us, always seeking to rise higher in expression and to fulfil Thy law through us all.

"We thank Thee, oh Great Spirit, for the opportunity to manifest to the children of earth the greater laws of the spiritual realms, so that, with their co-operation, we may be able to serve Thee and the world of matter by revealing Thy wondrous plan, so that the knowledge of Thy laws will enable all peoples to understand the purpose for which Thou hast placed them in the world of matter, so that Thy knowledge shall banish all ignorance. Thy strength shall drive away all weakness. Thy light shall illumine all the darkness and all suffering and misery shall be replaced by joy and happiness."

Chapter Ten

'EACH SOUL MUST GROW'

OVER the years many famous people made their way to the medium's London flat to hear Silver Birch speak. These included politicians, writers, artists, theatre personalities and reformers in such areas as animal welfare.

Once was present a Fleet Street editor. He put to the guide questions on the difference between thought and inspiration. Here is how the guide answered:

"You who live in the world of matter are most unoriginal creatures. You do not, except very seldom, create anything. You are receiving stations and also transmitting stations. Thoughts come to you; they lodge within you; you add to their wings and send them forth where others receive them. The thought that comes to you is not the same as when it leaves you; your personality has quickened it, or slowed it down, enriched it, or impoverished it, made it more beautiful, or more ugly, given it new life, or perhaps vitiated it. But over and above all that, you can, when you attune yourself, receive positive inspiration from those of like mentality to yourself.

"When people 'die,' as you call it, they come to our world, but all the richness of soul and mind which is theirs cannot die. It is divine, infinite, and like all things divine and infinite, it cannot perish. All the qualities of soul and mind continue to grow, to unfold, to develop and to mature in our world. The mere fact that you possess these great qualities of the soul means that when you reach this world of ours, you soon desire to render service to those less fortunate than you. You find, or strive to find, people like yourself.

"If you were a poet, you seek a poet; a musician, you seek a musician, like interests wherever possible, so that you can give freely all you have learned in your new world. The difficulty is to achieve the process of attunement. It is not our fault that inspiration is limited to brief flashes. If the laws that regulate conditions between the two states of life were perfectly understood, if the people of your world were to rid themselves of the many prejudices and superstitions which create barriers to a full and free communication, this wisdom of the infinite could be poured through human instruments into your world. It always depends on having an instrument to receive what we give and the ability of these instruments to attune themselves to receive the highest that can be given. All inspiration, all wisdom, all truth, all knowledge is dependent upon your capacity to receive."

The next question was, "I still cannot quite understand why these things should come in a flash."

"It is because at that moment you have attuned yourself and the chord of response has been struck," said the guide.

Answering another question, Silver Birch said: "It is very hard to draw the line. Often thoughts are not only sent to you and received by you from people in *your* world, but they also come from people in *our* world. There is a constant cycle of thought. Certain qualities attract certain thoughts. This process is going on all the time. But inspiration is a definite attempt on the part of someone, attracted by a similar quality, interest or calling, who is trying to give you what he has already achieved. Much of your music, poetry, writing and art is not born in the physical brain, but really originated in our world."

"How would you describe a genius?" was another question.

"You must appreciate that nature, or the law, whichever title you use, never evolves in one straight line," said Silver Birch. "There are variations, there are cycles, or even spirals of progress. Although you can clearly see the ascending scale of man's evolution from the amoeba to the spirit, there are often some who are in advance of their evolution and others who are behind it. You always had the precursors and the retrogrades. Your genius is the precursor of evolution. In centuries to come the whole race more or less will have evolved to what your genius is today. He is the advance guard."

Answering the comment that his conception was vastly different from earthly standards, Silver Birch said: "Always I approach things from a different standpoint. I see with the eyes of the spirit. I do not see with the eyes of your world. You cannot help considering all your problems in their physical aspects. You live in a physical world. You have physical difficulties to conquer, food, clothing, shelter. The very nature of your daily existence makes you cognisant of the world of matter in which you live. It is hard for you to approach all these problems from the standpoint of eternity.

"But we see you as spiritual beings, pilgrims on an infinite march. We know that your world in which you are living is not your eternal home. You pass through it for a few brief moments compared with the eternity in which you will live. Our focus is a much wider one. We view all your questions in the light of simple truths. What good will they do? How will they help others? What service will they render? All through the years I have used this instrument I have repeated, until sometimes I have felt I must get wearisome, that the truths we have to teach are very simple, that the only religion is the gospel of service. This is because we see truths which many do not.

"Millions of people think the world in which they live is the only world. They think the life they are living is the only life they will live, and so they try to accumulate all the things of matter, the earthly treasures which one day they will have to leave behind. The cause of your wars, bloodshed, misery, sickness—practically all of them—is due to the fact that the secret of life eludes millions who do not know that they are eternal spiritual beings here and now, that they are not bodies only. They are spirits expressing themselves through bodies. They are placed in a world of matter to grow and to develop that soul which will fit them for their real home which begins from the moment the Angel of Death touches them on the shoulder and says 'Come hither.'"

The guide's statements led to a discussion on evolution in which Silver Birch joined, saying: "All children are part of the Great Spirit, part of the process of infinite creation. They themselves help to determine the law of which they are a part. It is all part of the scale of ascending values. From the moment consciousness began to express itself there was spirit and a spiritual evolution began to take place. Physically, man has reached practically the apex of his evolution, but spiritually he has a long way to go."

When an author, whose name is known all over the world for his novels, attended the circle, Silver Birch said to him: "I do not like calling you stranger, because in reality, you are not a stranger to the power of the spirit.

"Yours is not a conscious exercise. Yours is the inner gift of the one who knows of the welling-up from within that cries aloud for expression, of words that demand to be used, of ideas that cry out until they are clothed with language, of the beauty that rises and seeks to envelop you, of a world which sometimes has puzzled you. Is that not so?"

"That is perfectly true," said the visitor.

"And yet," said the guide, "as I say to so many, in moments of reflection, when you have pondered on the processes behind life and have asked yourself the answer to the inevitable questions of how, why, where, you have seen the finger of destiny that has pointed the way in your own life, even from early childhood days. Is that not so?"—"That is true."

The guide went on: "We are always proud to welcome those who, in any fashion, enrich the world in which they live, who help to fill it with beauty and with joy, who bring comfort in any shape or in any form. But there is something far greater to be done than you have already achieved, and that I wonder whether you know."

"I should very much like to know," said the author. "But do you feel it?" asked the guide. "I do," was the emphatic answer. "You know he is psychic," said Silver Birch to one of the circle, who answered, "Yes, he has got 'psychic' eyes."

"But it is an untrained faculty. It is purely natural," the guide commented, and then, turning to the visitor, he said: "You do not know those who guide you. But they have helped you even more than you realise."

"What is it he has to do?" asked a sitter. "It is something much bigger than he has already done," said Silver Birch. "It will unfold itself, but he knows because it fills and pervades his being, and sometimes will not give him any rest. You understand me, don't you?" he said to the author, who answered, "Perfectly."

"Try to realise this," said the guide. "You, like all people in your world, have a large soul within a small body. It is a crude and clumsy way of expressing it, but you are compelled to express yourself through a body which is pathetically inadequate for the soul of which it is the medium. As you allow all the faculties of the soul, which is your true self, your reality, the abiding presence, as you allow all these talents and gifts and faculties to find expression, so they seek to escape from the thraldom imposed by the body.

"Because the soul is itself superior, even though it is temporarily encased by matter, so it devises ways and means of asserting its mastery and its supremacy, unconsciously, without any training or development. That is what has been happening to you. All the inspiration, all the activity, all the unseen side of you has temporarily burst the bonds and flooded and suffused your being and you cannot resist it. You understand me, don't you?" Again the author answered quietly, "Perfectly."

"But you have been assisted by those who are in my world," said the guide, "people whose souls are freed from the temporary limitations of the flesh body. They are tied to you by love, for love is the greatest tie in the world. Love naturally unites itself with its beloved, and there is no one, no power, no force that can separate love from its beloved. And those who love you, with all the wealth and warmth that love can bring, they help you because so much of what has happened could not be explained by you in your own expression of your life. But, in addition to them, there are others, greater in soul-content than your loved ones, with no kinship of blood, of family, but attracted for the reason of a common interest and a common purpose. They are the ones who have assisted far more than at present can be described and they will, at some time, if you will allow them, make themselves known to you."

And then the man who wrote books that sell by the thousand, books with a message of great beauty in them, replied: "I should be very happy to know them, and would you also thank all my friends on the Other Side?"

"They hear you," said the guide. "What I would like to be able to leave with you is the realisation of the closeness of the power which surrounds you. I am an old soul who has returned to this world because it was felt there was some work I could do, that the little knowledge that I had assimilated could be used to help people of your world. I have found many friends, many instruments to whom tasks were assigned."

When an American journalist visited the circle, his first question was, "What can you tell me about the spirit world?" No doubt because the guide heard one of the members of the circle declare that the journalist "would call himself a psychical researcher," Silver Birch began his answer by saying humorously:

"I am one regarded by your world as being dead. I am not

supposed to exist. I am a collective hallucination on the part of those who are assembled here today. I am a product of the medium's subconscious mind. I am his secondary personality, his multiple personality, or his split personality, whichever of these psychical research terms you choose to employ. But actually I am a human being, one just like you, except that I laid aside a long time ago the body of flesh through which you are manifesting today. That primarily is the difference between us. You are a spirit expressing yourself through a physical body. I am a spirit expressing myself through a body of spirit.

"I passed to the world of spirit, I 'died' roughly 3,000 years ago. That is a long time to you, but it represents very little in the span of eternity. I had made some progress. When you have been for some time in the world of spirit, still subject to laws of evolution, increasing the expression of whatever gifts with which the Great Spirit has endowed you, you make some headway, you move higher and higher through the planes of spirit life. I do not mean that there are separate planes of existence, each marked off from the other with fixed boundaries, but that there are grades of spirit life, each occupied by people qualified to exist in them. As, spiritually, you improve and progress, so you leave behind one plane of existence and merge into another. It is one long ascending ladder of progress with an infinite number of rungs.

"You can easily imagine after many hundreds of years you leave the world of matter far behind and have no desire to be in association with it. After all, it is not a very beautiful world. It is not filled with all the noble qualities expressed by the majority of the people who live there. There is much that is rotten and corrupt. There is much, too, which casts its dark shadows over human life and the sun of the spirit penetrates, alas, to but a few.

"When you live in another life where there is no economic stresses such as you have, where money has no value of any kind, where earthly riches do not count, where physical possessions are of no moment, where all are known for what they are, their only riches being the richness of their spirit, their only possession being the strength of their character; when you live in a world where there is no struggle for existence, where there is no exploitation, where there is no vested interest, where the weaker is not automatically driven to the wall, where all natural talents, however dormant, find their full expression, the world of matter seems very squalid and very unattractive. After many hundreds of years, I, with others, was told that there was a great need, that the world of matter required the help of beings like myself who could return, and perhaps impart some of the knowledge of spiritual laws which they had understood, so that a perplexed and weary mankind might be told how to find guidance and inspiration, and the solutions to problems which it found baffling.

"We were told that power would be given to us, power to quicken men's souls. But we were also told that it would be a hard task, that we would encounter many who would not look upon our mission with favour, even though they held high office in the churches of religions. We were warned that we would be regarded as emissaries of the devil, as evil spirits, misguiding, tempting, seducing men to paths of wickedness. In short, we were told that it was not an easy task, but a hard one, and, if I may add this, in order to accomplish it, we would have to forgo all the joys, all the beauties, all that we had earned through many long years. Yet not one refused out of all who were approached. And so, in company with some others, I come back to your world, not to live in it, but to work within its orbit. I had to find an instrument—always the hardest task. I had to learn your language and familiarise myself with your customs. I had to have an understanding of your civilisation.

"Then I had to learn how to use this instrument, so that I could say through him those few simple truths, so simple that they would revolutionise your world if all accepted them and lived their implications. At the same time I had to learn that, whilst working close to earth, I had to maintain touch with those who sent me, so that always I could be the mouthpiece for greater wisdom, for greater knowledge, for greater learning. It was very hard at first. It is not so easy now. Gradually I was able to reach those who were amenable. Not all welcomed the news that I brought—there were many who preferred to sleep. There were others who liked their little prison that they had constructed for themselves. They were safe in their cell. They were afraid of what liberty might bring them. But here and there I made friends. I had nothing to offer them except truth, reason, common sense, simplicity and the love of a fairly old soul who desired nothing for himself except to help any who might be brought to him.

"We have gone a long way since then, touching many souls. There are many who no longer are in the darkness of ignorance. There are many who have rescued themselves from the mists of superstition. There are many who have liberated themselves from prejudices. There are many who have gladly enrolled under the banner of freedom. There are many who no longer shed tears because now they understand the purpose of death and the meaning of life."

The journalist's next question was, "Do souls begin when men are conceived, or do they pre-exist?"

"Now you touch upon a matter of great controversy," said Silver Birch. "I can only speak for myself. Always I have appealed to reason and judgement. I have always said to those who hear me, if there be anything which I say which makes your reason revolt, which insults your intelligence, or which you cannot accept, then discard it, reject it. You will not hurt me; you will not offend me. I will love you just the same. Hannen Swaffer is as yet amongst the unconverted. The others, I think, have fallen to my wiles and believe in a pre-existence.

For myself, I say there is pre-existence, in many cases voluntarily undertaken for a specific purpose."

"I have never denied that," said Hannen Swaffer. "I only object to the idea that reincarnation is necessary for soul development."

"I am glad, then, you are with me at least part of the way," answered the guide.

"You told me once that I was reincarnated," Swaffer said. "I only deny that there is a law of reincarnation."

"May I point that whatever happens is according to a law," was the spirit reply. "Even voluntary reincarnation can only take place if there is a law. When I speak of a law, I mean a law which controls reincarnated birth into your world. We teach that everything in the whole universe, no matter how small or how large it may be, is controlled by law."

"Is it true that our difficulty in understanding time makes it hard for us to understand reincarnation?" queried the American guest.

"Let me put it another way, the way I always see it," was Silver Birch's reply. "You do not know *yourself*; you are unaware of that *you* which has never yet expressed itself in matter. You are only conscious of that infinitesimal portion which registers itself through a body of matter, but the real *you* is much larger than that which has ever manifested through your body. You, as you know, are not your body. You are a spirit with a body, not a body with a spirit. Your consciousness has an existence apart from your physical body, for example, in the sleep state, but that consciousness is not able to bring an awareness of itself through the limitation of a physical brain.

"And so you are able to appreciate only that part of consciousness which is expressed in matter. The larger part remains unexpressed, except in fleeting glimpses, until the processes of development enable you to become aware of the larger self. But, generally speaking, it is not until you have passed through the veil of death that you are able to come into that true inheritance which is your own. This is answering your question another way. The consciousness which you are now expressing cannot, through a physical brain, be aware of that larger consciousness until, either by process of development, or you have discarded the physical body, you begin to register that consciousness through a body which more properly can express it."

"You describe this world as being full of ugliness which does not exist in the world where you are," said the journalist. "Why is there this evil and ugliness in our world?"

Silver Birch replied: "We must differentiate between evil, or the lack of entertainment, as I prefer to call it, and the ugliness caused by the deliberate free will of those who have power to impose it and that evil and ugliness which is the result of man's imperfect development on earth. You must try to understand that a good deal of the ugliness and evil exists because of the vested interests of those who find it pays them to build slums, those who are interested only in the money that they can make, who are unconcerned with what happens to their brothers as long as they line their own pockets. The evil often results from the sordid conditions into which these people are plunged.

"But then you must remember that man is infinite, that the whole of life is a struggle from darkness towards the light, from the lower towards the higher, from the lesser towards the greater, that through evolution man's spirit is constantly rising. If there were no struggle, if there were no distress, then there would be nothing for the spirit to conquer.

"While there are the potentialities of the Godhead within man, it is only through development that they can be expressed. The process of development is like the extraction of gold. It consists in crushing, refining, purification. Ultimately you will rid your world of much that is called evil and ugly, but always there will be some betterment that is possible, for as man becomes increasingly aware of his innate divinity, so he becomes dissatisfied with the standards of yesterday and sets himself a higher standard for tomorrow."

The journalist commented that there "seems to be a conflict sometimes between the golden rule of doing things for your neighbours and the survival of the fittest."

"I do not believe in the way the law of evolution has been translated as the survival of the fittest, meaning the survival of the most ruthless in your world," replied Silver Birch. "The survival of the fittest means the survival of those with the fitness to survive. That means that those who have developed qualities of survival will survive. And you must remember, when you look at the animals who have survived, you will find that their survival is due, not to ruthlessness, not to their being the fittest, but because they co-operated with the law of evolution. If it were true that only the fittest survived, why are the prehistoric animals extinct? They were the strongest creatures, but they have not survived. The law of evolution is a law of growth. It is a law of unfolding all the time. It is a law of co-operation, service. In short, it is the law of the golden rule."

Answering another inquiry the spirit guide said: "The world is not ruled by chance; it is ruled by law and order. No matter where you turn, whether it be to attempt to comprehend the vastness of the interstellar spaces, whether you range with a telescope far over the horizons of the sky, or whether you take a microscope and begin to examine the small creations of life, all is subject to natural, unchangeable, immutable law. You are not the product of chance. Chance holds no place in an ordered universe where cause and effect follow one another with unalterable sequence.

"The power which fashioned all life provided rules or laws for its governance. It is perfect in its conception and organisation. These laws are spiritual laws, because all life is spirit. Life exists because its energy does not come from a world of matter, but because it is spirit. Spirit is life, life is spirit. Wherever life takes conscious form, there you have individual spirit. That is the difference between you and the lower beasts. Man is an individuated spirit, part of the Great Spirit.

"You either live your life as an individual, as a class, as a nation, as a world, in harmony with the law, or contrary to the law. If you live contrary to the law you get all the results, darkness, disease, difficulty, chaos, bankruptcy, misery, bloodshed. But if you live in harmony with the law you enjoy all the fruits of the spirit, all its wisdom, knowledge, understanding, truth, justice, equity and peace. That is what the golden rule means.

"You are not an automaton. You have free will, true, within restricted limits, but you have to make your decision. This is true of individuals and nations. Those who choose to live with the law, those who adopt the law of service to one another as their rule, automatically reap the results from nature and from the universe."

Asked about our attitude to our enemies—this was during the second world war—Silver Birch said: "To me all are spirits in bodies. I do not see Germans and Englishmen and Americans. I see spirits, part of the Great Spirit, and I know they are all part of His family. You may have to indulge in remedial punishment, but, as I have said before, you will not build a new world on hatred or vengeance. You will only build it on the desire to serve all mankind. Those who now shout, as they do, for reparation— an eye for an eye, a tooth for a tooth—are sowing the seeds of future warfare. There is room for all. There is enough for all, if all would solve their problems with reason and common sense. I could not make it simpler, could I? Why has America made progress in its short history? Because of one word—tolerance. And England has made progress in its long history because of its tolerance. You have solved in your country many of the problems of race, nationality, religion. You have almost solved the problem of colour. You have learned already through the history of your own country that all peoples have a contribution to make, and the addition of all their qualities produces, in time, the best individuals.

"What is already happening in your land must, in time, happen all over the world. You are seeing in miniature what is the solution to world problems. If you examine yourself, you will find it hard to determine all the strains that make up your being. Your country is none the poorer because it is composed of individuals of many strains; it is the richer. In breeding it is the constant addition and accumulation of new factors that produces the best results. It is so because nature thrives on the constant addition of new strengths, of new strains, for the infinite variation produces the best qualities. Nature is a restless march."

A Polish officer wanted to know, "Would it be true to say that only the people who see beauty in this world will be able to appreciate it in the next world?"

"No," said the guide, who went on: "It would be very unfair, for millions are unable to appreciate any beauty because they lack the educational facilities that enable them to have a true standard of appreciation. Our world is a world not only of retribution, but also of compensation, where all that you lacked in your earthly life is given to you so that a true balance may be struck."

The sitter who asked the question on the Pole's behalf commented, "What I think he has at the back of his mind is the fact that we take over to the Other Side those qualities we possess when we 'die.'"

"You must remember that you in your world are expressing only a small portion of an infinite mind," said Silver Birch. "This mind has only five windows and these are very inadequate. Once you are released from the body you begin to have a fuller expression. The mind is able to come into its own, for it now has a more perfect instrument through which to express itself. There are all kinds of beauty and the ability to appreciate beauty depends upon the individual's development. You can put two people together and show them the same sight. One will get from it richness and wonder, but the other will not. Then there is the other kind of beauty—beauty of the soul, beauty of the mind, beauty of the spirit, where one can derive deep enjoyment from the everlasting things of life. A well-stocked mind, contemplative, reflective, able to absorb the highest aspects of life, has a nobility and beauty all its own, something far removed from and inexplicable to those who have never appreciated it."

When the next question, "What is the best way to develop an appreciation of beauty?" was read to the guide, he replied: "Very largely the answer is that it is a matter of individual development. Granted that all reasonable educational facilities are available to all, the desire for beauty will automatically be expressed as individuals unfold. The higher your scale of values, the more your mind has grown, the more you will be dissatisfied with ugly, sordid surroundings, because they strike immediately a note of disharmony.

"It is always the first sign of evolution and growth when the individual wants to beautify his surroundings. All your striving to beautify the physical world is an unconscious expression of your own soul's growth. It is also part of your contribution to the work of creation, which is infinite. The divine mind has provided you with all the materials, many of them in their unfinished state, and it is the application of your soul, your mind, your reason, your intelligence, your growth that will help to bring perfection of beauty everywhere.

"It will always come back to the individual and his growth. The more he expands, the more he evolves, the more he allows the Great Spirit within him to find full expression, the more will he desire beauty. That is why I always insist on the moral and ethical implications of all this knowledge. Slums are wrong because the Great Spirit within you should not have to live in a slum. Starvation is wrong because the temple of the Great Spirit should be well cared for. All evils are wrong because they are an attempt to frustrate the expression of the Great Spirit within you. True beauty means true harmony everywhere, in all aspects of life, physical, mental and spiritual."

For his third question the Polish officer asked what he could do to instil into people's minds the idea of beauty. "Each soul must grow," answered the guide. "You can provide all the conditions and, if the soul does not desire to grow, you can do nothing. All you can do is to spread knowledge, driving out ignorance, driving out bigotry, driving out prejudice. Spread knowledge. Sometimes it will fall on stony ground, but very often it reaches receptive soil and the tiny seed that you have dropped will blossom. Our task is to spread the light wherever we can. Gradually the rays of truth will illuminate your world and all that belongs to the darkness of superstition, all that makes for ugliness and squalor will be transformed, as man desires to see conditions around him fit for the particles of the Great Spirit to dwell in."

'Done in Thy name'

"Oh, Great White Spirit, Who hast called us all into being. Who hast enabled us to come in Thy name and to gather up the power of Thy spirit and demonstrate Thy natural laws, we who are Thy instruments, render to Thee all thanks for the opportunities of service that Thou hast given to us.

"Oh, Great White Spirit, Thou art the light of all life, for without Thee there is darkness. Thou art the law which embraces all life. Because of Thee the stars are in their places, the sun shines, the flowers bloom, the birds sing. Because of Thee and Thy laws. Thy spirit is incarnated in Thy children of earth and they are linked with Thee. They are united with Thee and Thou dost express Thyself through them in all their desire to serve, to uplift, to rescue those who are fallen by the wayside, to give succour to the weary, drink to those who are thirsty and strength to those who are weak.

"Great White Spirit, greater and more majestic than the minds of Thy children can conceive, more filled with love and beauty and wisdom than the greatest of minds can comprehend, we know of Thee as the greatest and mightiest power in the universe, Who art the God of all gods, King of all kings, the supreme Law, perfect in its operation and its fulfilment.

"We pray that all that has been done in Thy name shall be filled with honour and with glory and we shall build here another temple of Thy spirit, filled with Thy power, radiant with Thy light, shedding its illumination far and wide, reaching all the dark corners of the earth so that there shall be in the world of matter a recognition of the Great Spirit and His eternal laws.

"We call to our aid all those of the larger life, of the higher realms, who, filled with power and knowledge, will help us to give to mankind greater understanding of Thee and themselves, that they may fulfil that destiny for which Thou hast placed them on earth."

Chapter Eleven

'REAPING THE HARVEST'

"WHAT is the power of the spirit?" the guide was once asked. "The power of the spirit is invisible," said Silver Birch. "It does not conform to any of the recognised standards of man. It has no length, it has no breadth, it has no height, it has no weight, it has no colour, it has no size, it has no taste, it has no smell. And so, by all the usual methods of calculation it does not exist, according to those purblind materialists to whom reality can only be appreciated when it comes within the radius of their five poor scales. Love is unseen and unheard. Love is colourless, without taste or measurement, but love is real, as those who experience its deep emotions can testify. But great as is the power of love, so infinitely greater is the power of the spirit.

"You live and move and breathe, you think and reflect, you decide and judge, you ponder and consider, because of the power of the spirit. You see and hear, you move and walk, you think and talk, because of the power of the spirit. All that you do, all that you are, is due to the power of the spirit, for your whole world of matter, and your body of matter, is dependent upon that vital, energising influx of spirit which gives it being, purpose, direction and life. Nowhere in the world of matter itself is to be found the secret of consciousness. Nowhere through the labours of the scientist, or the chemist, or the physician, is to be discovered the motive power of life. It does not reside within matter, for matter is but its temporary dwelling.

"The power of the spirit is the power that you call God, even though you do not understand what the term means, even though you have misinterpreted it and give it finite limitations. The power of the spirit is the power that breathed life into a world that once was all fire. The power of the spirit is the power which raised man up from the slime of the earth and endowed him with the qualities of divinity. The power of the spirit is the garment that the soul wears. The power of the spirit is the power which fashioned all life, which controls every motion and mutation of natural force, the power which regulates all the seasons and governs the growth of every seed, of every plant, of every flower, of every bush, of every tree, the power which is responsible for the whole scheme of evolution in all its intricate phases.

"It is a mighty force, the power of the spirit, for not only is it to be seen ceaselessly at work through myriads of material manifestations, but also in the higher realms of life, where it governs all spiritual activities, in worlds upon worlds whose existence at present is unknown to you, but where life is made manifest in forms far more radiant than anything known to you. But mighty as is that power, wondrous its many forms of activity, it has its restrictions, for it can be expressed only through vessels, through instruments, through intermediaries, channels, mediums—use what word you will. Those are the limitations placed upon its majestic flow. You determine the extent to which it shall be made manifest amongst you.

"You have always heard me urge you to banish fear, to radiate confidence, to live your lives upon a foundation of unyielding resolution, knowing that the power, the mighty power of the Great Spirit, would never fail you. It is because in such an atmosphere and in such conditions that it can the better operate amongst you. Earthly powers may fail and fall. Man's kingdoms are but transient. Those who now occupy high estate may tomorrow be classed among the lowly. But the kingdom of the spirit endures for ever. The nobility of the spirit is unchanging. The power of the Great Spirit can never wane. But you can, and do, determine the extent of its operation.

"Often I hear those who have knowledge say, 'Why has not the world of spirit done this or that?' when they themselves fail to provide the means by which the world of spirit could have fulfilled their requests. In a world that is full of anxiety, full of darkness and stress, be like beacons of light, so that, in their hour of trouble, men and women can come to you, attracted by the light of confidence that they see, and find a refuge and a sanctuary, a harbour of peace amidst the troubles of their days. You have the power to still the tempest of their mind and give tranquillity to their souls."

"At what time, as far as you know, does the spirit enter the body?" Silver Birch was asked.

"As spirit, *you* have always existed, because spirit is part of life and life is part of spirit," he replied. "*You* have always existed. Because *you* are part of the Great Spirit, which is the life-force, *you* have never had a beginning, but you as an individual, as a separate, conscious individuality, must begin somewhere even in the stream of life. When conception takes place, the cells of the male and female meet and provide a vehicle for a particle of the life-force to begin to express itself through a physical body. The life-force is unexpressed until there is a vehicle through which it can manifest. That is what the earth parents provide. From the time the cells have coalesced and formed their union, the tiny particle of spirit has naturally attached itself and begins its expression in your world of matter. And I hold that that is the dawn of consciousness. From that moment it begins its conscious individual life. Thereafter it will always be an individual entity of its own."

The next question began: "Through no fault of their own, innocent babies are born into the world victims of hereditary, venereal and other diseases. This does not seem quite fair, as it is not the fault of the child that it has inherited such a disease. Can you say something about that?"

The guide answered: "Those who talk of unfairness are still thinking in terms of bodies, of a world of matter, and not of an infinite life. The spirit does not suffer from venereal disease. The spirit is not crippled or misshapen or bent. The spirit is not suffering from any hereditary traits or any of the acquired characteristics of the parents. These do not change the individual, although they do affect the body through which the spirit manifests on earth.

"Whilst you can quite possibly argue that, from the earthly point of view, looking at life solely from a material standpoint, the one who is born into a diseased body has a much worse time physically than the one born into a healthy body, those opinions do not hold in regard to the spirit which is behind the body. You will not automatically be poorer in spirit because your body is diseased, and richer in spirit because your body is healthier. Indeed, it can be argued that your spirit will be richer because you will have learned the many lessons of pain and suffering which are all part of the equipment of the spirit in its essential evolution."

"What, then, is the urge to improve this world?" the guide was asked. To this Silver Birch replied, "The urge comes inherently from the free will which the Great Spirit has given to all children so that they can be co-sharers with the Great Spirit in His infinite creation."

This answer produced the comment, "If the spirit is improved by physical suffering, why do anything to alleviate it?"

"I am not advancing that," said the guide. "I am saying it could be argued so in order to demonstrate that there is infallibly a law of compensation at work. You cannot point to two bodies, one diseased and one healthy, and say because of those conditions the souls suffer accordingly forever. The lesson

I am trying to draw is that it is not the body which determines the state of the spirit. The spirit has its own path of evolution to tread. No matter what body is provided it always must be subservient to the twin laws of compensation and retribution."

Here someone interjected, "But it would always be better for the body to be born free from disease."

"Of course," was the spirited rejoinder. "It would be better that your world were free of slums, but slums are caused by part of that self-same free will which could enable your world to be a paradise on earth. If you have free will, then you must allow for its misuse and its correct use."

Another pressed his point by saying, "But it does seem that one would lose one's incentive to make the world better if one knew that suffering may help the spirit."

"There is nothing in your world that has not got its compensation," said the guide. "It would be a great mockery of divine justice if you could say that man has power so to thwart the Great Spirit that he could condemn the spirit and prevent it reaping the harvest which is its inherent right. I am pointing out that there is a law of compensation and that even were man working against the laws of progress, setting in force laws which are not in harmony with the laws of the Great Spirit, even when he has done all that, he has failed to thwart the divine plan, for there is a divine compensation.

"But it also must be pointed out that if you were to remove all the causes of present suffering, man, of his own volition, would still, out of the very complexity of his civilisation, introduce fresh causes which enable more suffering to take place. Life is a series of infinite gradations towards progress. You have to create steps one at a time, but do not think that the process of creating ever achieves a stage of finality."

"Disease of body may improve the spiritual evolution of the individual," stated one member of the circle, "but it can also do the reverse. It can worsen their character."

"Sometimes it does and sometimes it does not," said Silver Birch. "The case can be stated either way. You have disease because you break the law."

"Then you are surely stating that there must be disease or its equivalent," the guide was told.

"No, I do not say the equivalent of disease, but the equivalent of some suffering," Silver Birch declared. "You cannot have free will without having its pleasures and its pains. Surely you agree with that?"

"Yes," said the sitter, "because if there were no suffering, there would be no happiness. It seems to me that if you insist that there must be this, that or the other in place of something else, why worry about changing the world?"

"How else would you have it since man has free will?" asked the guide.

The answer was, "I would say, leaving out this terrible war, that the world today is much happier than it was 300 years ago, and in most countries, even with war, they are much happier now."

"Yes, but how does this defeat what I say?" inquired Silver Birch.

"We are always improving the world," the sitter replied.

"But there will be individuals with a desire to improve the world," said the guide, "because they are allowing their natural, divine, inherent talent to be expressed. It is because they are part of the Great Spirit. If tomorrow, by act of law, you introduced legislation which gave you all that you ask for today, it will not be satisfactory. The restless, evolving spirit will be dissatisfied, and rightly so, because it knows, within itself, that there is a greater perfection to be achieved. The suffering of today is largely due to man's abuse of free will. Always there are checks and counter-checks. Always there is progress and setback. There is an ascending evolution, always going forward and falling back. There are those in advance of their time and those behind their time. One rightly helps to push the backward ones forward, and the backward ones rightly act as a check on those who are too far in advance. There must be a constant striving for perfection. But do not lose sight of the fact that there is compensation all the while for all the miseries and misfortunes of life."

"There is so much to be righted," said one.

"There are millions in your world who, despite your much-vaunted boasts of freedom, are far from free," declared Silver Birch. "Look at all the coloured people, still regarded as inferior subject races, even by your own country which loves tolerance better than almost any other land in your world. That is why I always say that you should never be satisfied. The world could be much brighter, much fairer and much happier."

After Silver Birch had explained, from his viewpoint, the operation of natural law, these questions were sent to him: "If struggle and distress are essential for spiritual progress, are not these necessary in the next world? Yet you teach that there is no evil and ugliness in the Beyond."

The guide replied: "This questioner has not quite interpreted what I said. I said there were two kinds of evil—I never like the word 'evil'—and ugliness—that which was caused by the vested interests of the selfish and that which was due to man's imperfect development. There is no ugliness in our world, except in those very low spheres, of course, where dwell the people whose lives were so impoverished that they have no beauty to enhance their conditions here. But with that exception of the grey spheres, evil and ugliness have no existence in a world where the causes of evil and ugliness have been removed, and man's spirit is free to engage in those pursuits which are natural and necessary for its orderly development, growth and progress.

"Struggle and distress there will always be—but it depends how you interpret these words. There will always be a struggle in your world between the two forces which seek to control man, his animal ancestry, the force of the brutish beast that belongs to his physical evolution, and the divine spirit, the breath of the Great Spirit, which unites him with the infinite processes of creation. Man's free will decides in this constant struggle in your world which will obtain the mastery and succeed in holding it. When you come to our world, there is struggle, in the sense that there is a constant effort to overcome faults of the lower nature, to give rise to the higher innate qualities of the spirit; the struggle towards perfection, towards the light; the struggle in which you are discarding all the grosser elements of your being, as, strengthened, purified, refined and tested, the pure gold of the spirit gradually emerges.

"There can only be temporary distress in my world, because souls are dissatisfied with their progress. But these are only temporary adjustments, part of the long march of progress towards perfection."

Here someone interjected, "But always, in the other world, there is struggle, progress, and the need for effort."

"Yes," agreed the guide, "that is why I said it depends on interpretation. Always the higher seeks to eliminate the lower. It must be so, otherwise evolution would cease to be a truth. Man is a progressive being, growing from lower to higher states. In order to achieve growth he must constantly struggle towards the light, and that struggle is part of the process of growing. What I was trying to say was that there is a great deal of unnecessary struggle, a great deal of unnecessary striving, because man, by abusing his free will, has created needless conditions of squalor, disease and slums which make the task of the spirit all the harder in your world."

Then dealing with a further question, the guide said: "He wants to know if the Great Spirit is perfect. What does he mean by the Great Spirit? I can only deal with the Great Spirit as I regard the Great Spirit—the eternal, immutable, omnipotent, omniscient, natural law. I am not aware of any imperfections, faults or blemishes in that law. It is perfect in its sequence of cause and effect. It is perfect in the provision it has made for every aspect of a truly complex universe. When you consider, to take but one example, the myriads of creatures of varying sizes, shapes, colours and organisms, all of whom are provided with their sustenance by natural laws which overlook nothing, then you begin to see how truly comprehensive, how perfect in its conception and in its organisation is the law of the Great Spirit. To me the Great Spirit is the law, the law is the Great Spirit. The law is perfect, the Great Spirit is perfect. But you are living in an imperfect physical world.

"You who are living in physical bodies are at the moment expressing yourselves through finite minds, limited in their capacity to understand or appreciate even the world in which you dwell by your five senses of matter. These five senses determine the extent to which you can be aware of all that is happening around you whilst you are manifesting through a physical body. It is therefore impossible for you to grasp infinity. It is therefore impossible for you to understand perfection. It is therefore impossible for you to appreciate the Great Spirit or the operation of the Great Spirit's law, as long as you are restricted to your five senses. Though it may sometimes seem, because of your limitations, that the law is not perfect, with greater understanding and knowledge, viewing the same problem with the perspective of added wisdom, you do begin to realise that your former outlook was wrong.

"The world of matter is in a state of evolution. As part of that process, there are all kinds of developments, some quiet, some violent, which are part of the constant interplay of natural forces which are moulding the world in its growth. There are checks and counter-checks all the time, because you must have the two opposites in motion to produce the natural means of being. It is very complicated, I know."

"You say that we are part of the Great Spirit," interjected one sitter. "As we are imperfect, does not that say that the Great Spirit is imperfect?"

"No," was the answer, "because you have the seed of perfection, but that perfection cannot be expressed until you have the perfect means of expressing it. But your expression is at present imperfect. When you have evolved the perfect instrument, the perfect spirit body, then you will express perfection, but it will take infinity before you can do it."

"Will it also take infinity before every part of the Great Spirit reaches perfection?" the guide was asked.

"No," he replied, "the Great Spirit is perfect, but that portion of the Great Spirit which is at present expressed in human beings in a world of matter is imperfect, but it is struggling towards perfection."

"It is like an idea wrongly interpreted and used in an organisation; the idea is right," commented another sitter.

"Yes," said the guide, "but it has to be expressed gradually, stage by stage, getting better all the time as it approaches the ideal. It does exist, in the same way as you have always heard me say that you are expressing only a tiny fragment of the real you. If you were to judge the real you by the fragment that you express, you would really have a very poor opinion of yourselves. But that is only a small part of the real you. There is a larger you, a larger consciousness, which is still related to you, but it cannot express itself until you have provided it with the correct vehicle."

"That seems to get away from the idea of the Great Spirit as a single entity," a member of the circle said. "Is there a Great Spirit?"

"There is not a man seated on a great white throne," declared the guide. "There is not a person. There is a law."

"With a mind?" he was asked.

"Mind is not always restricted to bodies like yours," Silver

Birch said. "It operates through law. You must dissociate mind from brain matter. Consciousness is not focused in the grey matter and cells of the brain. Consciousness exists apart from the brain altogether. You must not think of mind in terms of your little brain box. Mind exists in itself. In order that you may be aware of mind, you must have a vehicle through which it can express itself for you. You have bodies so that you can express yourself. If it were possible to visualise a state where there were no bodies, you would still exist, but you would have no means of manifestation.

"It is hard to explain to you," said the guide, "because you can only think in terms of beings. It is impossible to explain in your earthly words that which is beyond words or symbols. You are dealing now with the stuff of creation. I cannot say there is a focalised force which is the Great Spirit. It is not that at all. The Great Spirit is the perfect mind, the perfect law which operates throughout eternity, without beginning and end. I cannot say that one day there was no light and the next day there was light. Life is a circle, without beginning and without end."

"Would you say there is as much of God in all of us as there is anywhere?" the guide was asked.

"The Great Spirit has no existence apart from the totality of the Great Spirit which is manifested in all creation," he replied. "Unfortunately, your world still retains this idea that creation began somewhat like the story of the Garden of Eden. It is not like that at all. There has always been a process of evolution at work; it is not that the universe had no existence and then it suddenly began to exist. The universe has always existed. Life in some form or another has always been made manifest, and life in some form will always continue to manifest."

Now here is what Silver Birch once said of spirit truth: "How fortunate are you to possess this knowledge which will enable you to give rich service to a world of darkness. How fortunate are you to possess the key to the many riddles which have puzzled great minds throughout the centuries. How fortunate are you to have the wisdom which will illuminate your pathway and make you understand your rightful place with the eternal, divine scheme of life. You should be proud of the knowledge that you have earned, for it will help you to rescue the many who are buried beneath the debris of false teaching, so that you can point the way to knowledge and understanding. And yet, how much greater is the responsibility that lies on your shoulders, for in truth you are standard bearers of the Great Spirit. You are the instruments of the most high. Upon you rests the responsibility of doing nothing that will dishonour or besmirch the sacred cause to which you are dedicated.

"Your world needs this knowledge, because it will illuminate the whole of life and make what was incomprehensible easy to understand. It will enable men to cease to be tortured by all the crudities and inadequacies of erroneous teachings that have for too long acted as a brake on progress. You are living in great times, for history is being written before your eyes. You are helping to shape its course towards that freedom which is the goal of every soul. You have a spiritual contribution to make. You have to disseminate this knowledge to ensure that the children of the Great Spirit everywhere are enabled to build on true foundations that will endure amidst all the storms and stresses of life everywhere. Those who oppose you are gradually dwindling in number. The formidable opposition of yesterday has become but a pale shadow today. The tasks which faced the pioneers of another age have now lessened, because of their labours. Yet there is much work to be done, and upon your shoulders falls some of this great task.

"Hold your heads high. Stand erect. Be proud of your contribution to freedom, to progress and to enlightenment everywhere. You are helping far more than you know to set souls and minds free, so that the children of the Great Spirit can dwell, not in the darkness, but in the light of truth. A new spirit is making itself felt. Men and women everywhere are turning their backs on old systems which have failed them in the hour of crisis. You see now how the old order has been shattered. There has been an acceleration in the amount of disrespect that is given to the old because it is the old. Men look for new formulas, for new systems of life. They turn their eyes towards the light. Their hope is pinned on a future from which they expect a great promise for the children who will come after them. Dissatisfied with the past, they yearn for this truth. It is for you to supply that need, to bring them into touch with their own beloved who will guide them, step by step, and enable them to acquire that knowledge and that power that will equip them in the tasks of reconstruction that lie ahead.

"Labels are losing much of their attraction in your world. For too long men have worshipped titles and names, but now they have become disillusioned. There is a new spirit, a spirit of inquiry, a spirit that demands to know truth, that does not believe in authority because it styles itself authority, that does not believe there is truth in the past just because it is the past and is supposed to be a record of divine intervention."

Advice on preparation for spirit communion was given in these words: "Learn to be passive, quiescent, receptive. You cannot command the power of the spirit. Its manifestations have to be prepared in orderly fashion. The transmission requires certain essential conditions. If you block the channel, the inspiration cannot flow, or else it becomes tainted. The great lesson to be learned is to keep your balance amidst all the turbulence and turmoil. If you have not absorbed that from our teaching, then some of it has been in vain.

"You are part of the Great Spirit with a vast reservoir of power on which you can draw. Amidst all the storms and stress, amidst all the noise and clangour, amidst all the chaos and confusion you can stand still and know that nothing can disturb the eternal, divine, infinite *you*. Difficulties have to be overcome. It is in the overcoming of them that your characters are moulded, that your spirits grow, that you find your real selves. There is much work to be done by all of us. This horrible war, this mass killing of bodies, this orgy of destruction, this sorrow that streams all over the world, creates great difficulties. But the war will not last forever. When it comes to an end, we can go forward again to accomplish the mission which is part of our lives."

Then in words which all the guides could address to their many instruments who are aiding the spirit plan, Silver Birch went on: "The work will be done as long as you are patient, sympathetic and understanding. I have spent a long time guiding your footsteps. I cannot begin to tell you of the many occasions on which I have whispered into the ear of your conscience to prevent you making false moves that would have led you away from the paths of service. After some labour which has ranged over many years you have been brought together so that the work can be done, the work which will teach the children who dwell in the world of matter how to order their lives so that their spiritual natures function as the Great Spirit intended that they should. That work will go on unless you decide of your own free will to turn away from the paths on which you now stand.

"We must use whatever talents the Great Spirit has implanted within us so that we can reach the largest number of people. At first we began with a few, but the trickling drops, as they collected, soon became a stream which in time will emerge as a mighty ocean. It has taken almost a century to arrive at the position in which the number of those who can say 'I know' are to be counted in all the lands. In another century, the numbers who will join the mighty ranks will be far in excess of those who are today still regarded as pioneers."

'In the rising and setting sun'

"Let us seek the blessing of the Great Spirit on the work that we are trying to do.

"Oh, Great White Spirit, Thou art the law that embraces all life, for Thou hast created all life and Thou dost sustain all life, and the whole universe exists because of Thee and Thy laws.

"Oh, Great White Spirit, Thou hast placed Thyself in all phases of manifestation. Thou art revealed in the rising and setting sun, in the ebb and flow of oceans, in the glittering stars in the sky, in the song of the birds, in the flash of lightning and in the roar of thunder.

"Oh, Great White Spirit, Who hast been worshipped by all peoples in all times and Who hast been presented according to the light of those who have beheld Thee, Thou art still greater, more mighty, more full of love, wisdom, justice, mercy and understanding than the greatest of Thy children of matter can realise.

"We who are Thy servants in the world of spirit seek to reveal those laws which have been hidden for so long and revealed only rarely to those who could pierce the fog of matter, see with the eyes of spirit and understand because they had the discernment of the spirit.

"We seek to bring Thy greater kingdom into recognition, so that Thy children may realise that they are not just alone, but spirit of Thy spirit, filled with Thee, part of Thee, with Thy strength and Thy light within them to resist and to conquer all evil and injustice, to enable Thy spirit to shine in their lives so that the world of matter may recognise Thee and the supremacy of Thy laws.

"We desire to work with all those who would uplift the weak, who would give comfort to the weary, who would bring light to those who are in darkness, who strive to resist all that prevents the fulness of Thy love being made manifest on earth.

"That is our task, and we would seek to co-operate with all those who work for Thee, Thy Kingdom, Thy light and Thy love."

Chapter Twelve

'TO SUSTAIN THE WEAK'

SADLY many once wonderful words lose their true meaning simply through being over-used and devalued. Perhaps love comes into this category. When asked for his definition, the guide responded:

"Love takes many forms, ranging from friendship founded on sympathetic attraction and mutual interest to the supreme heights where, without thoughts of self, it seeks to serve wherever it can.

"Love is a word which is misused in your world. Very often those who use it do not mean love at all. It is mistaken for the activities of the senses when there is only the desire for gratification of certain instincts. But love as I understand it is a part of the spirit stirring within, seeking expression when it realises its kinship with its divine creator. The greatest love is the love that has no trace of selfishness, that does not seek in any way to perform any action because it will bring some satisfaction to the individual. That is human love in its greatest aspect. It is the spirit that has enthused all who desire to uplift mankind, to help the needy, to sustain the weak, to fight the vested interests that prevent the unfortunate from extracting the beauty that life could offer them.

"All who, in their own land and in foreign lands, have sought with altruistic motive to raise the standard of mankind, to make it aware of its infinite potentialities, are exhibiting love in its finest form. There are degrees—when the same spirit animates a man or woman to serve the object of his or her affection. That need not be selfish; it can be unselfish. And there is the lowest kind of love, the love that is restricted, that desires to protect and help only the ones to whom it feels an attraction and feels no pity, no mercy, no sympathy and no compassion for strangers. Divine love covers the universe. It is love that has shaped its course, it is love that has regulated its evolution, it is love which is part of the divine beneficence, it is love which actuates all those advanced spiritual beings who, forfeiting all that they have gained by their attainment, return to your cold, grey, unattractive world to give service to those who need it."

Silver Birch was once asked how he "would explain the Great Spirit to children."

"That is not a difficult task," said the guide, "if the one who is to do the explaining has a clear conception of the power which is behind all life. For myself, I would point to the divine artistry of nature's handicraft. I would point to the stars, the diamonds in the sky. I would point to the glory of the sun, to the pale reflection of the moon. I would point to the whispering, murmuring breeze, to the nodding pines. I would point to the trickling stream and to the mighty ocean. I would touch every facet of nature showing how each is controlled by purpose, by law. I would add that where man has made any discovery in the field of natural life, he finds it comes within the orbit of law, that its growth is controlled and regulated, that it is part of one vast, intricate, yet harmonious pattern, that order reigns supreme throughout the vast universe, controlling planets and insects, storms and breezes, all life, no matter how variegated its expressions may be.

"And then I would say, the mind behind all that, the power that sustains it all, the force that controls the whole vast panorama of the universe and many other worlds that you have not yet seen, is what we call the Great Spirit."

The next question was, "Are people responsible for all their own thoughts?"

"I would prefer to say that, generally speaking, where they

are what your world regards as normal, they are reponsible for all their actions and that is the acid test," answered the guide. "It is what they do that is of supreme importance. Whatever they are, they have opportunities for service, for increasing their spiritual stature, for advancing the growth of their spirit. These opportunities are not restricted to the virtuous or to saints. They come to all people, and according to the way that you take advantage of these opportunities, or fail to do so, your spirit is strengthened or weakened."

"In the next world, we know that children grow up to become adults," said a sitter. 'But what about those guides who remain children for many years on earth, and also children who have been dead for 18 or 20 years who still return as children?"

Silver Birch replied: "I will come to the defence of the Topsies who never grow up. Your hard, bitter world condemns those who go on being children, and claims all the time that it loves the innocence of the child. Yet it objects to them when it chooses to persist in that form of evolution solely to help them. The advantages are very easy to understand. The child does not suffer from the inhibitions of the grown-up. It has a naturally fresh outlook on life. It is not beset by the many problems that perplex adults and therefore is the best channel for communication. The child can naturally perform this task because it has not so many of the intolerances and prejudices of the grown-up people to conquer. It starts off as a fresh, radiant being, willing to help, and is not troubled by all the problems that belong to the adult life. Because it is not worried by them, it can quickly hold on to those elusive vibrations that make for the success of spirit communication.

"But that child personality is only a personality voluntarily adopted in a large number of cases with a sole desire of aiding your world. If at any time it chooses to surrender its task, it can return to a higher sphere, there to take up its thread of the larger consciousness in which the child had lived. Do not condemn them; they are most lovable instruments of the Great Spirit whose only desire is to serve, a service they give willingly and freely because they think they can help those who are hurt or crushed by your world.

"In the case of the ordinary child who comes back after many years still as a child, this is done for recognition. When you are concerned with identification, you must remember that children would not be recognised unless they showed themselves in the form and with the characteristics and habits by which they will be known to their parents. But that is only a picture drawn for the medium to transmit. It is like the television thrown on the screen. The medium sees the picture that is thrown on to the screen of her mind and transmits it. With a voice medium, it is the same, except that instead of the process being a visual one, it is an oral one, moulded out of the ectoplasm. The voice which is moulded reproduces, as far as conditions allow, the voice the child had on earth."

"How would a child who had been brought up to be cruel to animals be treated on the Other Side; would it be given animals to look after?" was the next question.

The guide replied: "We would have to undo the earthly teaching by showing how animals have rendered great service throughout many years. The child would be taken to the varying animal spheres to see what they are really like when they are allowed to have contact with those who love them and understand them. Gradually, the false teaching would be shed as greater knowledge came to the child. And it would be shown that the effects of cruelty are not only to be observed on the animals, but on the one who performs the act."

Another member of the circle introduced a question by saying: "Many people when they pass on have no knowledge of the afterlife. They are in a sort of daze and do not know that they have passed on. Does that apply to children, or do they accept the new life instinctively?"

"It depends on the child's knowledge," Silver Birch replied. "If it has not been too tainted with the ignorance and superstition of your world, then its natural understanding, based on its natural psychic powers, will enable a natural appreciation to occur."

"Did the Great Spirit intend that some human beings should 'die' before they fulfilled their plan of life?" was the next point.

"The plan is always that you should enjoy a full expression on earth so that you shall be equipped for the greater life of the spirit," said the guide. "If fruit drops from the tree before it is ripe it is sour. All life that is forced to quit its body before it has achieved its maturity on earth is unprepared for the world of spirit."

"If a child 'dies' of an accident, was that intended by the Great Spirit?" the guide was asked. "That is difficult to answer, because always I have to say 'yes,' with qualifications," was the spirit answer. "The whole of life is controlled by law and the Great Spirit is responsible for law. But law works through human beings. Ultimately everything comes back to the responsibility of the Great Spirit. You can argue that if you do something wrong you are not responsible because the Great Spirit made you like that. But that is fallacious reasoning. It is true to an extent that He ultimately is responsible for the whole universe, because His power created it and His intelligence endowed it, but you have your intelligence. You have the power of reasoning. If you choose to put your head under a train it is no use blaming the Great Spirit."

"Will you explain 'infant prodigies'?" was the next query.

"There are three kinds," said Silver Birch. "Some are incarnated souls with a memory of past experience to help, others are mediums subject to spirit influence, albeit unconsciously, and therefore receptacles of much learning, wisdom, knowledge and truth from our world. In the third category are the geniuses who are the advance guards of evolution."

Another time a sceptic's viewpoint was put to the guide.

A critic of Spiritualism wrote: "There is one point about Spiritualism on which I have never been clear. What is the real object of it? Is it to make people believe in another world where their friends still exist, or is there any other object as well? From my own point of view I do not need anything to make me believe this as I have always known it; in fact, I cannot imagine how anyone could think otherwise.

"I cannot see that it serves any good purpose for, say, Mrs. Brown to receive a message (supposedly given through a *genuine* medium) that her son is well and happy, for example. I suppose it is comforting for her to know that, if she believes the message is genuine. If someone who means a lot to you is dead—well, they are dead. You cannot have their companionship, which is one of the most missed things. You cannot, for instance, spend a holiday together in Switzerland. You cannot go fishing with them or take a country walk on Sundays. Have you found from experience that these messages do give people comfort?

"Quite candidly I consider Spiritualism is rather 'playing with a very dangerous fire' except when handled by those who are sufficiently initiated. But I do not think it right to condemn something which means a lot to others without being sure of one's facts. Why do these spirit guides have such fantastic names, such as Silver Birch? Anything like this makes me shy away and be dubious. I suppose I have a very practical mind."

And this is the answer by Silver Birch: "At any stage of evolution it is preferable that you should walk in the light rather than the darkness; it is better than you should be armed with knowledge rather than that you should be swayed by ignorance. The pursuit of knowledge must always be one of the primary aims of all intelligent human beings. Otherwise, superstition, prejudice, intolerance, bigotry would become rife were there not the demand for knowledge to counter them and to force them to retreat. At no time can you halt and say, 'Thus far will I go and no farther.' Life is an endless adventure, an eternal quest, for its motive power, its driving force, is infinite. The infinite spirit requires an infinitude of time in order to accomplish its infinite destiny. There must always be the desire for education, for growth, for progress, for advancement, the attainment of the higher and the discarding of the lower.

"Knowledge is your priceless gift, for it enables you to survey your world with a compass to guide you. No ship sails without instruments to guide it. Human beings would be foolish to go through life without instruments to help them steer their proper course. Knowledge is always desirable; knowledge should always be desirable. The one who stops and says, 'I do not wish to know,' is in effect demanding that he should become stultified, decayed and rusty. You cannot stand still; you must either advance or go back. You are travellers on an eternal march. The life you are now living is but a small part of the life that you have yet to live. Ahead of you is a long, long road of progress.

"It is better that you shall be equipped, that you shall face the future armed with the knowledge that will help you to master its problems. Knowledge brings responsibilities; it is part of the law of compensation. You have added to your mental stock something that you never before possessed, but, on the other side of the scale, there is the responsibility of what you do with that knowledge. All we can do is to offer you the information we have gleaned, based on the operation of spiritual laws as we have learned from our own experience. That is the chief purpose of those who, like myself, come to teach your world so that it may be rescued from the morass into which it has fallen.

"Some are not yet ready for this knowledge. Some think it unnecessary; others have to be treated like children, given toys with which to play until they can be led on to the paths where their minds will be instructed. I want you to get a comprehensive picture of the plan that lies behind all spirit teaching. It seeks to dissipate the darkness which has surrounded your world for so long, that has caused all the horrors with which you are becoming painfully familiar. At the root of all your evils is to be found this ignorance of spiritual law. Do you not realise that, once the gospel of materialism and all the self-interest it teaches is exploded for ever, you have rid the world of its greatest curse? Look around your earth and see the signs—the misery, the sorrow, the sadness, the bloodshed, the chaos, the bankruptcy—all due to false materialism, ignorance of the spiritual law.

"Men have built their lives upon false foundations. Nations have tried to organise their policies on the principle of national self-interest. Dictators have risen and have become tyrannical, only because they have been subservient to the gospel that might is right. Do you not see how necessary this knowledge is, not only to the individual, not only to the nation, but to the whole world?

"Examine your own lives and see now much richness this knowledge has brought you. You know that you can never go back to the days when you were ignorant of this great truth. Despite all the difficulties in your world, it has given you a stay, a foundation, a base on which you can stand with fortitude, no matter what you experience. You realise you are not creatures of chance, playthings of caprice, but part of the Infinite Spirit with an infinite power on which you can draw. Your world is very sick; it is suffering from a dread disease. I am enunciating a cure. Once this truth becomes universally accepted, once people fully realise that there is a world beyond the one of matter, that they are personally responsible for the lives that they live, that there is an eternal law which operates with perfect justice, then you will have a new foundation for life."

Answering another question, Silver Birch said: "Spiritualism can teach you of your spiritual gifts, concerning which many people are profoundly ignorant, and help to unfold them so that they can be used for service. There are walking about your land many who could heal, many who could give the evidence that means so much to aching hearts. When you remember that, you see how important it is for knowledge to be spread. Ignorance is our great enemy, because it encourages laziness of mind and spirit.

"There are sincere people who have been fed on ignorance, who have been taught that faith, blind faith, is desirable to knowledge, who believe that we are really evil, who believe that all of you are misguided, that they are right because it says so in the book. That is the danger of ignorance. It creates a lazy, self-righteous, religious superiority based on a fallacy. It creates an inversion of the mind which makes the thinking so distorted that it cannot see truth even when it is presented to it."

Asked on another occasion what the Nazarene meant when he said, "Cast not your pearls before swine," Silver Birch replied: "What he had in mind was that you should not attempt to force great truth on unready souls. He did not mean that you should be afraid of rebuffs, because his mission was one long rebuff, but that where you find your efforts to spread knowledge, truth, wisdom, understanding, are treated with scorn and derision then you should withdraw and make no attempt to give beauty to those whose eyes are so hidden that they cannot see it."

The guide was also asked about his attitude to personal guidance from the spirit world. "Personal guidance is a truth," he said, "but you have to be careful how you explain to the interested but yet uninitiated how it happens. Otherwise it would seem to them that you gain an unfair advantage in life merely because you have access to spiritual power. After all, the foundation of this truth is not that it enriches you materially but that it enriches you spiritually, that it gives you a knowledge of laws and realities that provide a basis for a complete understanding of yourselves, the universe in which you dwell, and the Great Spirit, Who is the divine architect. Of course, the two states of life blend, merge and harmonise one into the other. It is not possible to draw a rigid line of separation between the things of matter and the things of spirit. There are, from time to time, constant reactions on both planes of life, for that which is spiritual is expressed in a world of matter and that which is material restricts and conditions that which is spiritual."

"The object of living here, I suppose, is to do away with those things that limit the spiritual," commented a sitter, "so that we express more of our spiritual natures through our physical bodies.

"Yes, that is the whole object of life on earth," said the guide, "so that you shall realise what you are. Those who vainly imagine that they are bodies of matter, and naught else, are living a great illusion, from which one day they will awake into a condition of stern reality. The awakening may come in your world or in mine. It is much better that it should come in yours, for there you have all the conditions which are easier for the growth, evolution and expression of your soul. You were meant, while living in your world, to give full expression to the body and to the spirit. It is equally as wrong to think only of spiritual things and neglect your physical obligations as it is to concentrate on the purely physical requirements and neglect your spiritual duties. There should be a perfect balance, so that you can be, as has been said before, in the world but not of the world; that your physical body should be cared for, watched over and tended, because it is the temple of the divine spirit, and that the spirit, which is in the process of growth and evolution, shall have opportunities for expressing growth and evolution through the body."

Here is a further selection from the hundreds of questions sent to Silver Birch.

"Would not it be best for all healers to be in perfect health themselves before they begin to heal others?"

"The answer is that of course it would be better if everybody enjoyed perfect health. But those who heal by the power of the spirit are like other kinds of mediums—instruments, that is, they transmit something which they receive, it passes through them. They are channels of distribution, they turn it outward, not inward. Their qualifications, their gifts, their powers, whatever form they be, allow them to act as intermediaries, mediums for the world of spirit, so that its vital, energising, dynamic, health-giving, sustaining influence can reach other beings. The fact that they themselves may be suffering from some bodily affliction does not necessarily restrict their ability to heal others. One is a psychic quality, the other is a physical defect."

"Does tranquillity and attunement to the inner force help us to maintain health? Does this apply to all ills?"

"It would apply if all men lived their lives in accordance with the natural law, if they had done nothing to infringe those laws to bring about disharmony between mind, body and spirit. It would apply if they started equipped with healthy bodies and not subjected to the disease of heredity. It is true that you, if you know how to tap the fountain of health within, could drive out the ailments which afflict the body, but since you have allowed disease and sickness to gain a supremacy, the task has become all the harder. There is a limit, for you have not the power to thwart death in its entirety. It is part of the natural law that when the body has served its purpose it shall be discarded, but unfortunately, in too many cases, the spirit has to pass unprepared, unripe and unequipped, because it has not enjoyed all the experiences which are necessary for it in its training. I can only expound the operation of the law. I do not say it is easy to accomplish what I have set out, for the whole mode of earthly life has been based on the supremacy of matter over mind and not mind over matter. The mind is supreme, the spirit is king, but the kingdom depends on your activity."

"What happens to the physical organism when this sense of tranquillity is achieved?"

"It is as it should be, made subject to the domination of the reigning spirit. It is controlled in all its intricate processes by the mind which occupies that body. It is at the direction of the spirit which creates all life and which has moulded the body through which it is functioning. You are asserting your supremacy, you are consciously exercising your superiority over every particle of which your body is composed. When you are able to do that, you have achieved a complete harmony so that every part is in complete concert with the other, all the rhythm is perfect, and you are at peace with yourself. There is no discord, no clash. Tranquillity rules because the spirit is at one with the Great Spirit of all life."

"How is it you are able to speak the English language so beautifully?"

"Your Western world adopts a curious attitude. It imposes as a spiritual test the ability to speak its language. It does not follow that, because anyone can speak English well, he is of necessity an evolved soul. It may well be that the one who addresses them in faltering language is far more evolved than they are. I have spent many years in learning your language, your habits, your customs. It is part of the principle of co-operation which is our natural life in the world of spirit. We give and take.

"If we wish to help your world we must learn its methods, some of which are indicative of the heights to which man can reach. Some of them are revolting and indicate the depths to which children of the Great Spirit can sink. As I had to address myself to the people who speak English, I had, after years of practice, to master its many difficulties. You have helped me and I have been also helped in my own world by those whom you have considered to be its masters. I am still helped now by many who achieved prominence in your history because of their beauty and simplicity of expression."

"Do our spirit friends hear us at all times when we mentally speak to them?"

"No, they do not. It depends on whether they are attuned to you or not. They can hear you if they are in tune. It depends on the vibrations. I am attuned to all of you. I can receive your requests whenever I desire to do so, for automatically when you send out a request the spirit vibration that it creates, the very ripple that it makes in the atmosphere, forms a pattern which is known to me. Wherever there is that kinship between souls in two states of life, then all the thoughts, all the requests, are immediately known."

"When people pass on, are there spirit doctors to care for them, both before the event and after it?"

"Yes, because they have to help the spirit body to release itself and to be prepared, as much as is possible, for its greater life. That is why, frequently, before death takes place, the ones who are to make the transition become aware of loved ones and strangers who are gathered around the bedside, helping the soul to free itself."

"In view of the conditions prevailing today, is it wise to bring fresh children into the world?"

"We teach personal responsibility. Though the world is filled with chaos, anxiety and strife, though the world is filled with bitterness, antagonism, and hatred, there is a new world which is to be fashioned out of all the strivings and miseries which are being endured. Some there must be who are to become its standard-bearers. The race must go on.

"The spirit must perfect itself through struggle, through difficulty, through labour. Humanity marches onward, not because it treads an easy path, but because it conquers all difficulty and emerges triumphant. Fear is always the worst enemy, for fear is born in the darkness of man's ignorance.''

'Thy spirit is within all'

"Oh, Great Spirit, Thou art the law behind all life. Thy smile is the radiance of the sun. Thy tears are the raindrops that fall from heaven to earth. Thy eyes are the stars that glitter in the firmament. Thy cloak is the mantle of night. Thy love is the desire within every heart to serve and to uplift.

"Thy spirit is within all things for Thou art everywhere. Thou art revealed in all the manifestations of nature. Thou art seen in the flowers that bloom. Thou art heard in the birds that sing.

"Thou art understood by all whose hearts are inclined towards Thee. Thou, oh, Great Spirit, Whose laws reign supreme throughout all the universe, always hast been and always will be. Thou hast revealed Thyself to those who can see with the eyes of the spirit.

"Thou hast taught them Thy love. Thou hast shown them Thy wisdom. Thou hast revealed, according to their understanding, Thy plan. Thou hast inspired all those who would seek to bring Thy kingdom on earth, so that they have gone forward with the courage born of the spirit that is within them to serve Thee by serving Thy children.

"Thou hast sent us Thy ministers to uplift and to comfort, to teach and to reveal, that those who co-operate with us are bringing to the world of matter a new light, a new knowledge, a new truth and a new wisdom that shall make the souls of Thy children free and that they may realise how much they are of Thee.

"We pray that in this temple the power of Thy spirit shall flow and, through it, there shall go forth into the world of matter a radiance of Thy truth that shall light up the dark places of the world and bring peace, happiness, knowledge and wisdom."

The Silver Birch Books

Teachings of Silver Birch	first published in 1938
Guidance from Silver Birch	first published in 1966
Philosophy of Silver Birch	first published in 1969
More Philosophy of Siver Birch	first published in 1979
Light from Silver Birch	first published in 1983
Silver Birch Companion	first published in 1986
A Voice in the Wilderness	first published in 1986
The Seed of Truth	first published in 1987
The Spirit Speaks	first published in 1988
Lift Up Your Hearts	first published in 1990
The Universe of Silver Birch	first published in 1994
The Silver Birch Book of Questions and Answers	first published in 1998

Spiritual Truth Press is the publishing arm of
The Spiritual Truth Foundation which is a charity
established to assist needy Spiritualists and Mediums as well
as to help to spread spiritual truths by financing the
publication of new and classic books on subjects relevant
to our understanding of man's nature and destiny.

All proceeds from the sale of this book will go to the
Foundation to further its work. To that end it welcomes
donations and bequests.

For further information about The Spiritual Truth
Foundation contact the Secretary at 15 Broom Hall,
Oxshott, Surrey KT22 0JZ